Object Lessons and Stories
for
Children's Church

Jessie P. Sullivan

BAKER BOOK HOUSE
Grand Rapids, Michigan

Sue Maberry

Formerly published under the title,
Children's Church Programs

© 1973 by Church Growth Publications, Inc.,
Nashville, Tennessee 37209

Reprinted 1974
by Baker Book House Company
ISBN: 0-8010-8037-1

Tenth printing, March 1990

PHOTOLITHOPRINTED BY CUSHING - MALLOY, INC.
ANN ARBOR, MICHIGAN, UNITED STATES OF AMERICA

CONTENTS

FOREWORD

Children's Church is becoming an important subdivision in Christian Education as educational leaders are realizing the benefits which come from the use of this very important morning hour for the spiritual growth of the children of the congregation. This formerly wasted time has become an exciting contribution toward the spiritual growth of boys and girls who not only learn to worship God on their own level, but enjoy it! Correlated with memory work and singing, the programs in this book will provide enough material for 26 complete worship programs.

As all workers with children know, the programs need to be varied and interesting. People who tell stories must practice them in order to tell them well. Relaxation, verses and songs interspersed with object lessons, and stories will provide an opportunity for variation, rest, and a change of posture. Boys and girls love to sing and participate in the program, and they appreciate an opportunity to move about and "perform." However, the very act of learning to remain in a designated seat for a definite period of time is one of the training aspects of Children's Church. Also, reverence is emphasized, especially by example. Boys and girls are anxious to please adult leaders whom they like, and they respond with pleasure when these adults appreciate their contributions.

As pointed out in *Children's Church Handbook*, (Baker Book House) (by Jessie Sullivan) our Children's Church is a little over an hour in length, and we follow an order of worship something like this:

> Organ or Piano Prelude
> Doxology
> Group Singing
> Welcome to Visitors
> Announcements
> Offering
> Scripture
> Lord's Prayer
> Object Lesson
> Special Music
> Application Story

i

Group Singing
Memory Work
Bible Story
Closing Prayer

There is no strict rule to follow the strict order of service, however, because variations are in order. Flexibility is a great asset when possessed by an adult leader.

When there is evidence of restlessness, relaxation exercises are fun and help to get the blood circulating in small bodies. Here are some that we use. Have the children stand and use actions.

I touch my head,
I touch my toes,
I touch my ears,
I touch my nose.
I touch my head,
I touch my feet,
I stand up straight,
I take my seat.

———————

Birds fly up,
Birds fly down,
They fly straight,
They fly around.
Birds fly low,
Birds fly high.
I'm not a bird,
So I can't fly.

———————

Up, up, up,
Higher than myself,
I reach my mother's Bible,
On the very top shelf.
Down, down, down,
I'm as careful as can be,
Handling the Bible
Spelled B-I-B-L-E.
Turn, turn the pages,
A memory verse I'll say.
 (Choose someone to recite a verse)
Up, up, up
I put the Book away.

Down, down, down,
In the basement I will see
If I can find
A B-I-B-L-E.
There's one back
On the tool table.
Tell me a verse,
If you are able!
(Choose child to tell verse)

————————

One last word—don't let the fact that you do not have a lot of adults available keep you from having a Children's Church. The attitude in which *you* start will determine how the children act. If the programs are interesting, discipline problems will be at a minimum. However, in order to have variety, and also for the sake of the time taken for preparation, there probably should be at least three leaders. We find that this is very sufficient in leading up to 40 children.

May the Lord bless you in this very rewarding work!

PROGRAM 1
GOD MADE US

Larger Scripture Lesson: Genesis 1:1-26

Scripture for Children's Church: Genesis 1:1-5, Genesis 1:26, 27

Object Lesson:

God Performs Miracles

Object: Transistor radio

We can't understand how God made us. Scientists have been working for years trying to discover how to make life. After all these years they still don't know how it is done. But just because we don't know how something is done does not mean that it can't be done.

Take this raido, for instance. (Play it.) None of us knows how sounds can be transmitted through the air and caught in a box right here in this room. We know it is possible, though, because we can see and hear it.

When God created the world, He created everything in it. Now man has learned how to use many of the things in inventions such as the radio.

We know that God created the world and everything in it because He said so. God has proved that His Word is true, so we can believe it.

Application Story:

Thank You, God

Bessie was in a hurry. She would be late for school if she wasn't careful. "Dear God," she prayed silently. "I'm sorry I didn't get up the first time Mother called me this morning. Please help me to be at school on time."

Bessie hated being late to anything. She knew that it interrupted her teacher when a boy or girl came in after the last bell rang. She knew that Miss Norris didn't like to be interrupted,

1

either. Besides, Bessie knew that Christians should always try to do the right thing. She knew it was right to be on time.

Running as fast as she could, Bessie crossed the street and cut through the park. When she reached the street on the other side of the park, she looked both ways. Seeing no cars in sight except for one in which a man appeared to be sleeping, she started to step off the curb. Suddenly, she pulled her foot back. A strange feeling had come over her. Don't do it, a voice seemed to say.

Whiz-z-z. Before she could blink an eye, the man in the parked car had stepped on the gas and had zoomed across her path. Bessie gasped. If I hadn't stopped, I'd probably be dead by now, she thought. She gulped. "Thank You, God, for not letting me get hit," she prayed.

Soon she had walked the three blocks to school. She reached the corner of the playground just as the bell rang. She prayed again, "Thank You, God, for helping me to get to school on time."

It seemed to Bessie as if God had helped her all day. He helped her remember what she had studied for the spelling test. He helped her to be patient when it took all the others so long to sharpen their pencils when she was the last in line. He even helped her to pay attention while the teacher taught the history lesson.

That night Bessie was talking to her mother. "You know," she said, "God helps in a lot of ways. I never really thought about it very much until I decided I'd just notice special this one day. He helps *me* so much I don't see how He has time for anybody else!"

"That's one of the very wonderful things about God," Bessie's mother explained. "He can do everything and be everywhere at the same time. It's hard for us to understand, but the Bible says that God is a Spirit. Because He is a Spirit, He can be everywhere. He's not confined to a body like yours or mine. If He was, He couldn't do all the things that He does. Why do you suppose He takes such good care of us, Bessie?"

"Well, Miss Brown said in Sunday School that God made us. I guess if He made us, He feels like He should take care of us. He loves us, too. That's another good reason."

"Then why do you suppose everyone doesn't love God when He's so good to us?"

"Probably because they don't know Him," Bessie answered. "If they knew everything He does for them they couldn't help but appreciate it. I know there are lots of kids in my class who don't go to Sunday School or church. They probably don't even think about how good God is to them and how much He loves them."

"That's a shame, isn't it? Isn't there something you could do to help them to know more about Him?"

"Well, I could talk about Him more," Bessie answered. "And I can invite them to go to Sunday School and church with me."

"That's right. Why don't you try and see if it helps?"

"I know something else we could do, too!" Bessie exclaimed after thinking for a minute. "Why can't we have a Bible class here at our house? We could have it on Saturday mornings or one evening after school. Could we do that, Mother?"

"Why, I think so, but who can we get to teach it?"

"Maybe Miss Brown would come. She told us about Bible classes that people have in their homes. That's the way the first churches were started. Maybe she'd know how to do it."

Soon Bessie was busy making plans for her Saturday Bible Class. The first thing she did was to call Miss Brown on the telephone. She said she'd be delighted to come over at 10 o'clock the next Saturday if Bessie would have her friends there.

Bessie was busy all the rest of the week. She called and invited all her friends at school and all the neighborhood children, too. She helped her mother clean the house and bake cookies. Friday night, before she got into bed, she knelt beside it. "Dear God," she prayed, "please may all the kids come to the Bible class tomorrow and learn about You. Thank You for all you have done for me, and thank You for showing me a way *I* can do something for You!"

Bible Story:

Creation

God was alive before time began.

The Bible tells us that God "always was" and "always will be." It's hard for us to understand because we think of everything in relationship to time. Everything we do, even when we are very young, is done according to minutes and hours and days and weeks and months and years.

When we start to school, there's a time to get out of bed, a time to eat breakfast, a time to leave, a time to come home. While we are at school we are on a schedule. We have certain classes at certain times. We eat lunch at a certain time. If we didn't follow a schedule, our lives would be utter confusion. No one would

3

arrive at the same time. The teacher would be frantic trying to teach all the things we need to learn.

It's different with God. He is what is called "eternal." He always was and He always will be. He was not born like we are. He will not die like we have to die. He just always was and always will be!

Many thousands of years ago, God created the sky and the earth. The earth was shapeless and dark and covered with water.

God said, "Let there be light," and there was light.

God looked at the light.

"It is good," He said. "Now I will divide the light from the darkness." God called the light "Day," and He called the darkness "Night."

On the second day, God looked at the earth which was still covered with water and saw that there was a mist all around it. He cleared the sky so it could be seen and made the air, or atmosphere. He called the blue sky "Heaven."

On the third day, God said, "Let the waters be gathered together and leave some dry places." God called the dry land "Earth," and the big bodies of water "Seas."

Then God said, "Let the earth have plants on it. Let all of the plants have seeds so more plants can grow from these seeds. Everything that grows on the earth will bear fruit after its own kind." So plants grew on the earth. There were trees and flowers and grass and vegetables and herbs. Each one of these plants had seeds so more plants could grow from them.

On the fourth day, God looked at the earth and the blue sky. He saw the dry land, the seas, and the plants. He decided that there should be lights in the sky. "Let there be lights in the sky," He said. "These lights will divide the day from the night. They will also provide a way of telling time." So God made two big lights, one for the day, the sun, and one for the night, the moon. Then He made smaller lights to shine at night, too. These lights He called "Stars."

On the fifth day, God looked at all the things He had created —the earth, the air, the sky, the seas, the plants on the earth, and the sun and the moon and the stars. He said, "Let there now be fish to live in the water and birds to live in the sky."

Immediately there were all kinds of living creatures in the water and many kinds of birds in the sky.

God blessed them. "It is good," He said. "Now, may all of these fish and birds be fruitful and multiply. Each kind of fish and each kind of bird will have fish and birds just like themselves."

On the sixth day, God saw that He had created the earth and heavens, the seas, and the dry land and air.

He saw the plants growing in the earth.

He saw the fish swimming in the seas.

He saw the birds flying in the air.

"Now," He said, "let the earth have all kinds of living creatures. Let there be animals and insects. Let everything multiply by bearing young just like itself."

So, just as God said, there were many animals and insects on the dry land.

Up until this time, there had been no need for rain for the plants of the earth. And there was no one to till the ground so the plants could grow. So God caused a mist to come up from the earth which watered all the ground.

Then, on the sixth day, God created Man.

"Let there be Man, now," He said. "He will be like Me because he will be able to think and feel and he will have the ability to choose right from wrong. He will be in charge of all the fish and birds and animals and insects. He will be in charge of the whole earth."

So God created Man in His Own image. He formed him out of the dust of the earth. He breathed His own breath into Man's nostrils. The man became a living soul.

On the seventh day, God rested.

He had made a perfect world and had placed a perfect man in it to take care of it. He was very pleased.

PROGRAM 2
GOD IS ALWAYS WITH US

Larger Scripture Lesson: Exodus 1, 2

Scripture for Children's Church: Exodus 2:2-4

Object Lesson:

God Is A Trinity

Object: A hard boiled egg

I have an egg here. We've all seen eggs before. As a matter of fact, we all have eaten them. We can eat scrambled eggs, hard boiled eggs, soft boiled eggs, and poached eggs. Sometimes an egg is all mixed up in something, like a cake or a meatloaf. But it doesn't make any difference how you prepare it, an egg is still an egg.

When you look inside an egg, you can see that it consists of three parts: the shell, the white, and the yolk. (Cut the egg in two.) If you separate them, you don't have an egg. You have only a part of an egg.

With a cake of ice it is different. The ice is composed of three parts, too. But each part is *all* the ice, but in different forms. You have the cake of ice itself, the water that it can melt into, and the vapor which rises from it. All three are really the ice, but in different forms.

And so it is with God, because God is a "Trinity." "Trinity" means "three." God is a Trinity, because He is composed of three parts. He is God the Father, God the Son, and God the Holy Spirit.

When we talk about one part of God, we still know that there are two more parts, and all three are God. Because God knows everything and can do anything, all three parts of Him know everything and can do anything. We know that God and Jesus are both in heaven right now because the Bible tells us so. The Holy Spirit is here on earth with us. In fact, when we accept Jesus as our Savior and become Christians, the Holy Spirit comes right into our hearts. When He comes into our hearts we know that He will always be with us.

Application Story:

God Is Always With Us

Mary perched on the edge of the hard straight bench in the train depot. She felt pretty big most of the time, but today she felt more like a very little girl. For you see, Mary was sort of frightened. When her parents had told her she was going to travel on the train to Enid, Oklahoma, from Kansas City all by herself, she had thought it was going to be lots of fun, but now she wasn't so sure.

The big waiting room seemed dark and lonely to her, and she and a man sitting across from her were the only people in it. The emptiness made the large room seem even bigger. The dim lights made it seem scary, too. Mary wished that the announcement of her train departure would come over the loudspeaker soon. She wanted to get going on her way again.

When she had left Kansas City, her mother had told her she would have to change trains at Springfield, and it sounded like a very easy thing to do. Now that she was here waiting for her next train, she wasn't so sure. She looked at the big clock up on the wall and saw that it was 7 o'clock. Her train should be here in 15 minutes.

The man across the room got up and looked at his watch. He smiled at Mary, but she acted like she didn't see him. Her mother had always told her not to talk to strangers. He started to come toward her, but Mary looked away. What can I do, she frantically wondered to herself. Where can I go? She looked over to the other side of the long room at a ticket window where a man was sitting behind bars that formed a sort of cage around him. He was talking on the telephone.

Mary got up from the bench and started toward the ticket man. "Dear God," she prayed silently, "please help me. I know that man is just trying to be friendly, but I'm scared."

The man was moving slowly toward her. Mary knew he was following her. She walked faster. Was he walking faster, too, or was it just her imagination? She tried to look at him out of the corner of her eye, but she couldn't tell where he was. She was almost running when she finally reached the ticket window.

The ticket man had hung up the phone and was now looking

at her. He looks like a nice man, Mary thought. I'll ask him to help me.

Mary took a second look at him. "Oh!" she thought, "he frightens me, too. What can I do now?" She looked to both sides and saw no one else in the waiting room. There was only Mary, the ticket man, and the man who had been following her.

"Which way do I go to catch the train to Enid?" she asked when she reached the window. She already knew because the conductor on her last train had told her, but she had to say something.

"Over there to your right, Miss," the man answered. "Are you all alone?"

"Oh, no," Mary answered. "I'm never alone. God is always with me!"

Mary surprised herself with the way she answered, but it was true. She really wasn't ever alone, even now when she had almost forgotten. She looked at the ticket man. He looked like he had been surprised, too.

"You're a mighty fortunate young lady," he said. "I hope you have a pleasant trip. Oh, by the way, this gentleman behind you is a conductor. His name is Mr. Adams. He's in charge of the train you'll be riding. He'll take good care of you, I'm sure."

Mary looked up at the man who had joined them. He was smiling and he wasn't scary looking at all now. Just then the loud speaker sounded out. "All those now leaving for Tulsa, Enid, and Oklahoma City will now board on Track 3."

"Come along, Miss. That's our train," the conductor said. "This looks like it's going to be a fine trip. Tell me what you know about God. I've never heard anyone speak like that about Him before. Maybe you can teach me a few things. I've not gone to church much, and you make me think maybe I've missed out on something."

Mary was glad that God had taken care of her. There were lots of things she could tell the conductor about Him. "I think I'll tell him about Jesus first," she thought. "That will be a good way to begin."

Bible Story:

God Is With Baby Moses

The Israelites were living in the country of Egypt. So many Israelite babies were being born and were growing up that the Egyptian king became worried.

"We must be wise about this," he said. "We must see to it that the Israelites do not become stronger than we are. If we're not careful, they may soon become powerful enough to take over our government and make slaves of us. Let's beat them to it and make them slaves."

The king then set taskmasters over all the Israelites and made them work very hard. But the harder the Egyptians made the Israelites work, the stronger the Israelites became. Harder and harder they worked; stronger and stronger they became.

Then the king of Egypt tried something else. He called together all the women who were nurses for Israelite babies. He said, "When you see an Israelite baby girl, you can let her live. But when you see an Israelite baby boy, you must kill him."

The Hebrew nurses were afraid of the Egyptian king, but they were more afraid of God. They couldn't kill the little baby boys. They knew that God wouldn't want them to.

This made the king angry. "Why have you not obeyed me?" he asked.

"We have tried to," they answered, "but the Israelite mothers won't let us get close to their little boys."

The number of the Israelites continued to grow.

Now the king made another commandment. This one was to all the people. "Every baby son that is born to you must be thrown into the river, but you may keep your baby daughters."

Amram and his wife, Jochebed, heard what the king of Egypt commanded. They were frightened. God had given them a little baby son. They couldn't throw their baby son into the river. They loved him too much. They prayed that God would help them save their little boy. They hid him in the house as long as they could, but when the baby was three months old, he was getting too big to hide in the house any more. They were afraid that the soldiers would hear him crying and come in and kill him.

Jochebed decided that the best thing to do was to build a little waterproof basket that would float. Then she would put the baby into it and let him stay in the river. Maybe the soldiers wouldn't find him there. She made the little boat and daubed it with slime and pitch so it wouldn't leak. It was a perfect little boat to put the baby in.

"Come, Miriam," Jochebed said to the baby's big sister when the little boat was all finished. "Bring some blankets to make your little brother comfortable and warm."

They put the blankets in the basket and laid the little baby in on top of them. They looked down at him. He smiled and waved his hands and feet. He acted like it was fun to ride in the little boat!

Jochebed and Miriam went down to the riverside and very carefully put the little boat down into the water where some plants called bullrushes were growing. The little boat rocked and rocked. The little baby couldn't see outside the basket because Miriam and Jochebed had put a cover over it.

"You stay and watch your little brother," Jochebed told Miriam. "See that he doesn't get hurt."

"I'll do my best," Miriam said as Jochebed went back to the house. Then Miriam went off a little way to watch to see what would happen. "Little baby brother must be asleep," she thought, because he is very still.

Soon Miriam heard voices. She slipped farther back among the bushes so no one could see her. She peeked out to see who was coming. Why, it was the daughter of the king himself! And she had some of her maidens with her. Miriam waited to see what they were going to do. The princess went down to the river to wash herself. When she got there, she saw the little basket and said to one of the maidens, "Go see what that is over there among the bullrushes."

The young lady went over and picked the little basket up out of the water and took it over to the princess, who pulled the blanket off the top and looked in.

The little baby blinked in the sunlight and began to cry.

The princess looked at the little baby. She took him out of the basket and held him close to her.

"There, there," she said. "It's all right. I won't let anyone hurt you. I shall call you Moses because I have taken you out of the water." When Moses heard her sweet soft voice, he stopped crying. He liked the way she held him and rocked him back and forth.

"This must be one of the Israelite's children," the princess said to her maidens. "They've hidden him here so the soldiers couldn't find him."

Miriam, who had come out of her hiding place to where the princess and all her maidens were standing, said to the princess, "I know an Israelite woman who can take care of the baby for you."

"Go. Bring her to me," the princess said to Miriam.

Miriam ran home as fast as she could. Her heart was beating fast and she was breathing hard. "Mother! Mother!" she called. "Wait until you hear!"

"Tell me! What has happened to the baby?" Jochebed asked.

"Oh, Mother. Something wonderful has happened. The princess has found him and wants to keep him for her very own. I told her I knew a nurse who would take care of him, and she sent me to get you. Isn't that wonderful?"

Jochebed hugged Miriam. "Oh, Miriam, you have done exactly the right thing," she said. "Let's hurry back to them. God has been good to us. He has saved our baby."

PROGRAM 3
GOD FORGIVES

Larger Scripture Lesson: Genesis 1, 2, 3

Scripture for Children's Church: Genesis 2:15-17

Object Lesson:

Forgiving Others

Objects: A glass of clear water, iodine, ammonia

Forgiveness is when a person you have hurt or done something bad to tells you: "It's all right. I don't hold it against you any more. In fact, I've forgotten all about it."

You can forgive someone who has hurt you in the same way, by telling them that it's all right and that you won't remember it.

When God forgives us, He forgets all about the bad things we have done, too.

But before God can forgive us, we must do something.

We must be sorry for what we have done. We must be so sorry that we won't do the bad thing any more. Or, at least we'll try very hard not to.

After we have thought about it and have realized that we have done something wrong, we must ask God to forgive us.

George liked to tease his sister. He liked to do things that bothered her. He really wasn't mean. He just liked to hear his sister cry. Darlene was always crying when George was around, because he teased her constantly.

One day George stuck his foot out in front of Darlene. She didn't see it, so she tripped and fell down on the rough concrete sidewalk. She skinned her knee so badly that she had to go into the house to ask her mother to wash it and put some medicine and a bandaid on it.

"Darlene, I'm sorry I tripped you. I didn't mean to hurt you. Forgive me for not being a nice brother," George said.

Darlene believed that George was honestly sorry, so she

answered, "That's all right, George. Let's just not think about it any more."

If George was really honest when he said he was sorry, he wouldn't trip Darlene any more, would he?

When we do bad things, God is unhappy—things like taking something that doesn't belong to us or telling things that aren't true or not obeying our parents or being mean to a brother or sister—we should tell God that we are sorry. Of course, we really have to BE sorry, because God knows if we really mean it or not.

Let's look at this glass.*

It represents your life when it has no sin in it.

The only problem is that everyone has sinned or done something bad in his life. God's Word says, "All have sinned and come short of the glory of God."

This is how sin muddies up our lives.**

When our lives are dirty, God is unhappy. But if we are truly sorry for the things in our lives that make them so dark and ugly, we can ask God to forgive us. We can ask Him to let Jesus come into our hearts.***

Then, when we have Jesus in our hearts as Savior, He cleans all the sins out of our lives.

First: We must realize that we have sin in our hearts.

Second: We must be sorry because we don't measure up to what God wants us to be.

Third: We must ask God to forgive us.

Fourth: We must ask Jesus to come into our hearts to cleanse us from sin.

  * Hold up glass of clear water.
 ** Pour some iodine into the clear water.
*** Pour some ammonia into the dark water and watch it clear up.

Application Story:

Lost In The Big City

Ronnie was lost. He was lost in the big, strange city where he and his family were visiting Aunt May. About a half an hour before, he had gone for a walk to look around the neighborhood. He had been so interested in the many new and different things to see that he had completely forgotten to pay attention to where he was going. Now he couldn't find his way back to Aunt May's.

Ronnie was frightened. He wasn't used to the big city. He didn't know what to do. He sure wished he knew Aunt May's address. He really was in trouble.

He sat down on the curb. Putting his elbows on his knees, he rested his head on his hands. He closed his eyes. "Dear God," he prayed. "I guess I'm lost. Please show me how to get back to Aunt May's."

When Ronnie raised his head and opened his eyes, he noticed a little girl walking along the sidewalk. She was hugging her doll tightly with one hand and rubbing her eyes with the other. She looked as scared as Ronnie felt!

"Hi!" Ronnie said. "Is something wrong?"

"I can't find my mamma," the little girl sobbed. "I don't know where my house is."

"Don't cry, little girl. What's your name?"

"My name is Katie Keller and I live at 2016 Cypress."

"You're smart. It shouldn't be too hard to find your house, Katie. Come with me. My name is Ronnie."

Forgetting his own trouble, Robbie concentrated on helping his little friend. "Dear God," he prayed silently, "please help me to find Katie's house. Thank you. Amen."

Ronnie reached out his hand and Katie trustingly laid hers in it.

"Come on, Katie, at least we know what your address is! Let's find someone who knows where Cypress is."

Soon Katie and Ronnie met a nice lady carrying a sack of groceries.

"Excuse me, Mam," Ronnie said to the lady. "Could you tell us where Cypress Street is?"

"Why, yes. It's the next street over. Go to the corner, turn to your left, and walk one block. That's Cypress."

"Thanks a lot," Ronnie said. "That sounds easy enough. Come on, Katie. You're practically home!"

Ronnie and Katie hurriedly followed the nice lady's instructions. Sure enough, the street sign said "Cypress."

"Lookie! Lookie!" squealed Katie as she let go of Ronnie's hand and started running down the street. "There's Mommy!"

"Oh, Katie, where have you been? I've been looking all over for you," Katie's mother scolded. She stooped down and hugged the happy little girl.

"I was lost, but Ronnie helped me find you. Didn't you, Ronnie?" Katie said.

"That was very nice of you, Ronnie," Katie's mother said.

"Oh, it wasn't any trouble, Mam. She knew her address and that helped a lot."

Just then Ronnie noticed a house down the street.

"Why, there's Aunt May's house!" he said. "I have to go now. Good-bye!"

Ronnie skipped toward the house. He was glad he had helped Katie. The way it turned out, in helping Katie, he had helped himself! God had answered both of his prayers at once!

Bible Story:

Sin

Can you remember something wrong or bad that you did this last week? Something that you did last night, or maybe even this morning?

Have you ever taken something that didn't belong to you? Or have you ever disobeyed your mother or father or teacher? Have you ever told somebody something that was not true? These things not only displease people, they displease God.

Anything that displeases God is a sin.

And sin is in the world today because of one man who disobeyed God. His name was Adam.

When God created the world, it was like a beautiful garden. God made the Day and the Night and the sky. Then, because the world was covered with water, he gathered some of the water up into certain areas and made dry land in other places.

"Now," He said, "let the earth have vegetables and flowers and trees." And there were vegetables and flowers and trees.

"Let there be lights in the sky," God said; and He made the sun to shine during the day and the moon and the stars to shine during the night.

"Now," God said, "let the waters have fish and other living animals in it, and let there be birds to fly in the air."

Then God made all kinds of animals and insects.

When God had finished making the world and the sun and the moon and the stars and had put living things in the sea and in the air and on the dry land, He said, "Let us make man so he can rule over all these things that I have made."

So God made Adam.

God placed Adam in a beautiful garden. He said to him "There is one thing I do not want you to do. Do not eat of the fruit of the tree of the Knowledge of Good and Evil which is in the middle of the garden."

15

Then God made a companion for Adam; her name was Eve.

The Garden of Eden was a lovely place for Adam and Eve to live. They had everything they needed to be happy and comfortable. Every evening God came to the garden and walked and talked with them.

But one day a serpent came to Eve. He said, "Has God said that you can't eat fruit from every tree?"

"Oh, we can eat fruit from every tree except one," Eve answered. "But God has told Adam that we will die if we eat any of the fruit from that tree.

"Surely you won't die," the serpent said. "Why don't you try some?"

Eve went over to the tree. The fruit looked good. "Um—m—m," she said.

She picked a piece of fruit off the tree and ate it. Then she went to Adam. "Look, Adam, how lovely this fruit is. You eat some of it, too."

Now Adam knew that he should not eat any of the fruit, because God had told him not to. But Adam disobeyed God. He took a piece and ate it.

As soon as they had eaten the fruit, Adam and Eve both knew that they had sinned. They realized that they had disobeyed God.

That evening, when God came to visit with them, they tried to hide themselves. But God, of course, knew where they were hiding. God knew what they had done, because He knows everything.

"Have you eaten fruit from the Tree of the Knowledge of Good and Evil?" He asked.

"Yes," Adam answered, "but it was Eve's fault. She gave it to me."

"It wasn't either my fault," Eve said. "The serpent told me to eat it."

God was very unhappy because Adam and Eve had disobeyed Him. He was angry with the serpent, too.

God said to the serpent, "From now on you will be cursed. You will crawl around on the ground for the rest of your life. Some day I will send a Savior for my people. You have caused them great sorrow, but they will have another chance to be pure and good."

God said to Eve, "You shall have babies and many sad things will happen to you and all the women that follow you."

To Adam He said, "Because you have disobeyed Me, Adam,

you have brought sin into the world. Everything will suffer because of you. The ground will have weeds. Animals will kill one another. You will have to work for your food and shelter. There will be sorrow and suffering. And because sin is now in the world, death is also in the world."

"But," God said, I will make a way for the people to escape from death. I will send a Savior. If anyone will believe in Him and accept Him, that person will have eternal life."

Adam and Eve were very wicked because they disobeyed God. But in Romans 3:23 God says, "All have sinned and come short of the glory of God." That means that you and I have sinned, too, and we come short of the glory of God just like Adam and Eve.

Remember what God told them? He said that He would send a Savior to save the people from sin. That Savior is Jesus. Anyone who accepts Jesus may have eternal life.

We must look to God and Jesus and accept their gift. "For God so loved the world that He gave His only begotten Son that whosoever believeth on Him should not perish but have everlasting life" (John 3:16).

PROGRAM 4
GOD FORGIVES US

Larger Scripture Lesson: Luke 19:1-10
Scripture for Children's Church: Luke 19:1-4
Object Lesson:

God Forgives Forever

Object: **Cookie**

I have a cookie here. Everyone of you can see it. When we do things that are wrong or bad, God can see us and He knows what we are doing. Sometimes we think that we can hide our sins. And sometimes we can hide them from people. But we can never hide them from God, because He not only can see us, He knows our hearts.

There is only one way to get rid of our sins, and that is to be sorry for them and to ask God to forgive us for them. God will forgive us if we ask Him. The sins will be to Him just like you had never done them. Your sin will be just like this cookie. (Eat cookie) As far as God is concerned, it is gone forever!

Application Story:

A Telephone Call Helps Two People

Ted Wilson raced into his house, blood streaming from the cut on his chin. "Mom! Mom!" he called. "Where are you?"

Dashing into the bathroom, he turned on the cold water, soaked a clean wash cloth in it, and pressed the cloth to his chin.

"What in the world has happened?" his mother asked. "Here's let me see."

She took the washcloth away long enough to see the gaping wound and realize that she'd better let the doctor take care of it. Quickly, she rinsed the bloody cloth and placed it back on Ted's chin.

"Here, hold it tight, Ted. We'd better get you right to the doctor. It's lucky your dad left the car home today."

Ted pressed the cloth so the bleeding would stop and listened while his mother dialed a telephone number.

"Hello. Please let me speak to Dr. Goodrich," she said. Then, "Dr. Goodrich, this is Mrs. Wilson. Ted has had an accident and has cut his chin rather badly. Could I bring him down to you right away? At the hospital? We'll be right there. Thank you so much."

Mrs. Wilson hung up and grabbed her purse. While she was fishing for her car keys, she said, "Come on, Ted. Dr. Goodrich said for us to come right to the emergency room at the hospital. He'll meet us there."

The freckles stood out on Ted's pale face. He was afraid to talk for fear that the bleeding would get worse. He followed his mother out to the car and climbed into the front seat beside her. As they rolled out of the driveway, he noticed some of his friends who had gathered on his front walk. Charley Fisher was among them, looking almost as pale as Ted.

He looks scared, Ted thought. It serves him right. If he hadn't stuck his old foot out and tripped me, this wouldn't have happened.

It didn't take long to reach the emergency room of St. Luke's Hospital. Evidently Dr. Goodrich had already informed the waiting nurse about Ted, because she said, "Come right this way, please," almost as soon as they reached the door.

Ted and his mother followed the nurse into the examination room.

"Lie up here, please," the nurse instructed Ted, pointing to the examination table.

Dr. Goodrich rushed in just as Ted had taken his place.

"Well, well. It does look like you had an accident, Ted. We'll sew you up and you'll soon be good as new."

Deftly the doctor washed his hands and got to work. He cleansed the wound and proceeded to stitch it up. Ted winched, but tried not to move. I'm too big to act like a baby, he thought.

"I think he'd better spend the night here," Dr. Goodrich told Ted's mother. "He has lost a lot of blood and we don't want him to go into shock."

Ted felt rather important when the orderly rolled in a cart to take him to a room. He didn't feel too good, but he wasn't so sick that he couldn't enjoy the attention he was getting!

Soon he was settled between the cool white sheets of the hospital bed. After his mother went home he was grateful for the chance to take a little nap. For some reason or other, he was rather drowsy.

Soon he heard the rattle of dishes on the hospital trays and he was glad to see the young nurse's aid who brought him his tray. The food wasn't as good as his mother's, but Ted was hungry and ate it all.

After the aid came for his empty dishes, he lay back in the bed. He began to think about his friends, especially Charley. "I bet Charley is worried when he hears I'm in the hospital," Ted thought. "I bet he thinks something awful is wrong with me. I hope he's not too worried, though."

During visiting hours, Mr. and Mrs. Wilson came to see Ted.

"I'm fine. Really I am," Ted insisted. "Just a little wobbly. Say, could I have a dime? I want to call Charley."

Mr. Wilson felt in his pocket and pulled out some change. Picking a dime out of the coins, he handed it to Ted and they both walked down the hall to the public telephone. Ted dialed Charley's number and listened to the ring on the other end of the line.

"Hello?" a voice answered.

"Hello, Charley?" Ted asked.

"Yes. This is Charley. Who is this?"

"This is Ted. I just thought. . . ."

"Ted? Is it really you?" Charley interrupted. "Are you all right? I've been scared silly. I heard you're in the hospital. I sure didn't mean for you to get hurt when I stuck my foot out like that. I was just playing."

"Oh, I know it. It's all right. That's why I called. *I didn't want you to worry.* I *am* in the hospital, but I'm coming home tomorrow. Why don't you come over and see me after school?"

"Say, that's swell. Thanks for calling, Ted. You sure took a load off my mind!"

"See you tomorrow. Bye!"

Ted hung up the receiver and looked at his dad. "It could have happened to anybody," he said. "I feel a lot better now that I've called Charley. I guess that phone call helped both of us!"

Bible Story:

Jesus Forgives Zacchaeus

Zacchaeus was a rich man. He had a lot of money. He lived in a beautiful house and had many servants. He dressed in beautiful **robes.**

But Zacchaeus did not have many friends. He was dishonest and cheated people. Zacchaeus was a tax collector. He forced the people to pay higher taxes than they owed. Then he gave part of it to the Roman government and kept all the rest for himself. Everybody hated tax collectors. They hated Zacchaeus most of all because he was the chief tax collector.

Zacchaeus had heard about Jesus. He had heard how Jesus made sick people well, how He helped crippled people so they could walk, and about how He healed blind people's eyes so they could see. He had heard that Jesus would talk with tax collectors, too.

One day Zacchaeus heard that Jesus was coming to Jericho. He wanted to see this wonderful man who said He was the Son of God. He left his house and started down the road. He walked and he walked. He kept looking for Jesus because he didn't want to miss Him. After a while Zacchaeus saw a big crowd. He knew that crowds followed Jesus wherever He went. Jesus must be in that crowd.

Zacchaeus ran to where the people were. He tried to see Jesus, but he had a problem. He was very short. No matter how hard he tried, he couldn't see over the heads of the peopde.

He had another problem, too. The people saw who he was and they pushed him away. They didn't like him and they wouldn't make room for him.

He ran around on the outside of the crowd, trying to find a way to see Jesus, but there was no way.

Then he had an idea!

He had noticed a big sycamore tree back down the road. If he could get to that tree before the people got there, he could climb it and look down over their heads. Then he would be able to see Jesus!

Zacchaeus turned around and started running. He ran as fast as he could. Finally he reached the tree. He climbed up and sat on a branch. He looked back down the road. Yes, there they were. Jesus and the people were coming.

He watched the crowd approach him. He was excited. Now he could see Jesus! Oh, he was glad he had had this idea!

Then Jesus did something that surprised everyone. He walked away from the crowd and came over to the sycamore tree. He looked up at Zacchaeus. Zacchaeus looked down at him. Jesus looked good and kind.

He spoke. "Zacchaeus, hurry and come down. I am going home with you!"

He could hardly believe his ears! Jesus had called him by name! And He wanted to go home with him! He scrambled down out of the tree.

The people mumbled among themselves. "He's going home with a sinner," they grumbled.

Zacchaeus felt honored that Jesus had chosen his house to visit. He also felt bad because if Jesus knew his name, he also knew what a bad man Zacchaeus was. Zacchaeus was very ashamed.

When they reached Zacchaeus' house, they took off their sandles and the servants washed their feet. The road had been dusty.

"Bring some food," Zacchaeus told his servants.

"Here, lie down and rest," he said to Jesus, as he pointed to a couch.

Then Zacchaeus said something else to Jesus. He realized now how evil and dishonest he had been. He knew that if he was a follower of Jesus that he would have to change his ways.

He said, "I'm sorry for all the dishonest things I have done. Please forgive me. I'm going to give half of everything I own to the poor. And besides that, I'm going to return everything I have taken away from anybody. In fact, I'm going to give them four times what I took from them."

Jesus was happy. Zacchaeus had done more than let Jesus come into his home. He had let Him come into his heart.

PROGRAM 5
TRUSTING GOD

Larger Scripture Lesson: Job

Scripture for Children's Church: Job 1:1-3, 6-12

Object Lesson:

Things Happen To Us For Many Reasons

Object: Crutch (or cane—any implement to denote illness)

A long, long time ago many people believed that if bad things happened to you it was a sign that you had done something wrong and you were being punished for it. It is true that God has to punish His children when they need it, just like your mother or daddy has to punish you when you need it.

This crutch reminds us that people have accidents and they get sick. Sometimes these accidents and illnesses happen because we are not careful or because somebody else is not careful. Sometimes it's because we need to suffer to become more grown-up in our feelings and in our thinking. Sometimes it is because we are disobedient.

When we have troubles we should thank God for them and not feel sorry for ourselves. We should make the best of them and be glad that God will always help us if we ask Him, because He loves us.

Application Story:

The Baseball Banquet

George's big brown eyes flashed. "Come on, Larry!" he yelled.

Larry was trying to beat the ball to homebase. Thud! the ball hit the catcher's mit and bounced away. Larry was safe. "That's three runs for us," George said as he marked his tally sheet. Then he yelled to the boys on the team, "We're ahead now! Let's keep it that way!"

George was small for his age, but his voice rang out above the others. He loved baseball and never missed the chance to watch a game. His one big ambition was to have a baseball of his own with the autographs of all the Royals, their hometown professional team, on it. He would much rather play, of course, but several years earlier he had been sick with polio. The brace on his right leg was a constant reminder of the handicap it had left him.

But George didn't sit around feeling sorry for himself. No, siree! He did everything he could, and then watched the other boys do the rest.

George enjoyed being umpire when his team practiced in the park, and he kept score when they played a league game. He was always cheerful and the other boys considered him a part of the team even though he couldn't play. They got so they never noticed his brace or his limp, and they missed him when he couldn't show up for practice or a game.

When the game was over, all the boys gathered around Mr. Fritts, their coach. He had told them that he had some important news for them and they were curious to find out what it was.

"Some of you fellows may know about the banquet the Royals are going to have this week. Its purpose is to honor all the boys in the city baseball leagues, but since they can't have everybody because there wouldn't be enough room, they have asked that each team choose a representative."

The boys all started talking at once. Of course, they all wanted to go! Just think! Whoever went would get to see all the Royals in person and close up, too, George thought. He maybe would even talk with some of them. It was a cinch he'd get some autographs! Wow! What a chance!

George knew he wouldn't get to go, of course, but he was as excited as the others.

Mr. Fritts started to talk again and the boys became quiet. "You can be thinking about it tonight and we'll vote on it tomorrow. Okay! It's time to go home! See you after school tomorrow!"

The boys began to scatter and George got busy collecting balls and bats and bases and took them over to Mr. Fritts's car. Larry gave him a hand so they could walk home together.

"Good night, Mr. Fritts," the two boys called as they left the park.

Even though they were the best of friends, George and Larry were quite different. Larry was several inches taller than George. His walk was straight and erect, in contrast to George's limp. Larry had straight blonde hair and clear blue eyes, and George's hair was dark brown and curly and his eyes were brown. In spite of their differences in appearance, though, they both felt the same way about baseball. They both loved it dearly.

"Boy! I wonder who'll get to go to the banquet," Larry said. "That sure would be something, wouldn't it?"

"It sure would!" George agreed. "I'd like to be the one to get to go, but I guess I'm really not one of the team, so I shouldn't even hope. But I'd sure like to get the autographs of all the Royals."

"You're just as much a part of the team as anybody!" Larry argued.

"Well, I hope you're the one they choose," George said. "After all, you're the pitcher."

"See you in the morning," Larry called when he reached his house, which was next door to George's.

"Yeah," George called back as he went into his own house. When he got inside, he limped over to his desk to turn on the lamp. "Hi, Mom! I'm home!" he called to his mother who was working in the kitchen.

Looking at the clock, he saw he had some time to work on his homework before supper. He sat down and pulled out his list of spelling words. He tried hard to concentrate, but he soon had to admit that he was thinking so much about the Royals' banquet that he couldn't think about his spelling words.

"I might as well wash up for supper," he said to himself. "I can see this isn't doing any good."

After he washed his hands and face he joined his mother in the kitchen. Soon he was telling her all about the banquet. "And one of the boys from our team gets to go," he finished.

"That's nice, George," his mother answered. "Who do you think it will be?"

"I hope it's Larry," George answered, wishing way down deep in his heart that he himself would be the one who would be chosen.

The next night after practice Mr. Fritts took the vote. He had brought a piece of paper and a pencil for everybody so they could take a secret ballot. Each boy took his paper and pencil and went off by himself. Soon they had all returned the papers with a name written on each one. Mr. Fritts took the tally.

One for Larry, one for George, one for Dick, another one for George, another one for Larry. When he had counted them all out, Dick had two votes, Jeff had two, Victor had three, George had five, and Larry had six.

"Well, I guess it's Larry who gets to go," Mr. Fritts said. "I think you've made a good choice. I'll pick you up at 5:30 tomorrow afternoon, Larry. And there'll be no practice tomorrow, boys."

That night when George and Larry went home, George was happy that Larry had been chosen, but to be really honest, he was a little disappointed, too. Even though he'd known he didn't have a chance, it would have been great to have been chosen to go.

Later he told his mother, "Larry is my best friend. I'm glad he gets to go, if I can't." And he really meant that.

The next evening George stood on his front porch and waved good-bye when Mr. Fritts picked Larry up. "Bye!" he called. "Have fun!"

While Larry was gone, George tried to keep busy. He kept reminding himself that he really was glad that Larry was at the banquet. One time he prayed, "Dear God, help Larry to have a good time. And help me not to feel disappointed because I didn't get to go!"

Around 8 o'clock George heard a car door slam. He limped to the front door and got there just in time to hear Larry call, "Thanks, Mr. Fritts. I had a great time!" Then George heard footsteps running up his front walk and up onto his porch. He opened the door.

"Hi, George!" Larry said. "Look what I brought you!" He tossed his friend a ball, and when George looked at it he could hardly believe his eyes! It had the autographs of the whole Royal baseball team on it!

"It's for me?" he asked.

"Yeah. After all, I got to go to the banquet. I figured you ought to get something, too!"

George slowly turned the precious gift around and around. This was even better than getting to go to the banquet. He'd be able to keep the ball forever, and the banquet was already over.

He grinned and said, "Thanks, Larry. You're a real pal."
Bible Story:

Job

Job was a good man who lived a long time ago in the Land of Uz. Job loved God very much and he did everything he could to please God. He was very rich and lived in a big house. He had seven sons, three daughters and many servants. The Bible says that he owned 7,000 sheep, 3,000 camels, 1,000 oxen, and 500 donkeys.

One day Satan and some of his angels went to see God in heaven. Satan bragged about how powerful he was on earth. He claimed that he controlled more men than God did.

"Have you noticed my servant Job?" God asked. "He is a perfect and upright man who loves Me and turns his back on you."

"Yes, but no wonder," Satan answered. "Look at all You have given him. You've blessed everything he has done. Look at how rich he is. If you would let all these things be taken away we'd soon find out how faithful Job is. He'd probably hate You then."

God answered Satan. "We shall see. Do what you will with him," He said. "I know he could lose all these things and still love Me. Just one thing, though. You cannot hurt his body."

Then Satan left the presence of God.

Soon after, a messenger came running to Job. "Oh, Master," he cried. "The Sabeans have killed all your oxen and donkeys and the servants who were looking after them. I was the only one who escaped!"

While he was still talking, another servant came running up to Job. "Oh, Master, a great fire came and burned up all your sheep and your servants who were taking care of them. I am the only one who escaped!"

And while he was still talking, another servant came running up. "Oh, Master," he cried, "the Chaldeans have slain all your camels and the servants who were taking care of them. I am the only one who escaped!"

And while he was still talking, still another servant came to Job. "All your sons and daughter were eating together in your oldest son's house and a great wind came and knocked the house down and killed all your children and their servants. I was the only one who escaped!"

Job could hardly believe it. In just this short while, nearly everything that he owned had been destroyed. He was very sad. He got up and tore his cloak and shaved his head, because this was the way his people expressed their grief. Then do you know what he did next? He fell down on the ground and worshipped God!

"The Lord gave and the Lord has taken away," he said. "Blessed be the Name of the Lord!"

After all this, Satan went to see God again.

"Have you seen how loyal Job has been to Me even though you have taken away so many of his possessions?" God asked.

"Oh, yes," Satan answered, "but let him be physically hurt and he won't love You so much. Why, he'd curse You to Your face if that happened!"

"We'll find out," God said. "I'll let you hurt his body. But you cannot take his life. You cannot kill him."

Soon Satan caused terrible sore boils to come on Job's body. The sores were all over him. They hurt. They covered him from his head to his feet.

"Curse God and die," Job's wife told him.

But Job still remained loyal to God.

Then three friends came to visit him. Their names were Eliphaz, Bildad, and Zophar.

Eliphaz, Bildad, and Zophar went to see Job to try to make him feel better. At first, they didn't even recognize him. He looked terrible. They felt very sorry for him and sat down beside him and didn't say a word. They sat like this for seven days and seven nights.

Then Job broke the silence, "I wish I'd never been born," he told his friends. "I am so miserable."

Eliphaz answered him. "We all think that you must be guilty of something bad because we feel that God wouldn't let you suffer like this unless you had done something very wrong." Bildad and Zophar nodded their heads in agreement.

"That's not true," Job said. "I have done everything to please God. I have been a good man. I haven't done anything to deserve all of this."

"Surely if you had been so good and upright God would not let these things happen to you," Bildad said.

"But I haven't done anything wrong," Job insisted.

"How can you claim to be perfect?" Zophar asked.

"I know as much about God as you do," Job said. "And I've not done anything any worse than any of you. Even if God takes my life I will trust Him, but I will also defend my ways."

The three men continued to talk to Job and argue with him.

"You certainly aren't any comfort to me," Job said. "But God is wise and great. I may not understand why all of this has happened, but I will stand by God as long as I have a breath of life in me. I have shared with the poor and have been fair with my neighbors. I have been good to the fatherless. I have done nothing evil."

Then Elihu, another man, talked to Job. "You are self-righteous," he said. "You are not giving God the credit for yourself and your uprightness. You think you've done it all by your-self."

The men didn't realize it, but God was right there, listening to all they were saying. Now God Himself talked to Job.

"Who are you to say you are so good? He asked. "Did you create the world and the moon and the sun and the stars? Did you create the animals and the birds? Can you make it rain or hail or snow? Can you count the clouds? Do you make all the beauty in the world?"

"Oh, God!" Job cried. "I am truly unworthy in Your sight!"

"You have lowered Me in justifying yourself. You have claimed you have done nothing evil or wrong. But you have not given Me the credit I deserve."

"Oh, I am so sorry," Job said, and he really meant it.

Then God spoke to Elphaz. "I am angry with you and your two friends," He said. "You have not spoken of Me correctly, like Job did. Go now and take seven bulls and seven rams and go to Job and offer up a burnt offering to Me. I will accept Job's prayers for you."

Eliphaz and Bildad and Zophar did as God told them, and He forgave them of what they had said against Him.

God forgave Job, too. And not only did He forgive him, He gave him twice as much as he had before. He gave him seven more sons and three more daughters, the same number that he had had before.

And he doubled his animals. He gave him 14,000 sheep, 6,000 camels, 2,000 oxen, and 1,000 donkeys.

Job lived 140 years after this experience, and he always re-membered how God had shown him how very holy He is. He remembered that he could always trust God. He had learned that just because you suffer doesn't mean that you have sinned, but sometimes God lets a person suffer to help him become a better person. And now Job was a better person.

PROGRAM 6
JESUS LOVES US

Larger Scripture Lesson: Matthew 3

Scripture for Children's Church: Matthew 3:16, 17

Object Lesson:

God Knows Us

Object: Tape recorder (Record something in front of the children and play it back at the appropriate time.)

Sometimes we don't realize how important it is to always tell the truth. Oh, we know it is wrong to tell a lie, but for some reason or other we go ahead and do it and think that we can "get by" with it. But we don't "get by" with anything. Sometimes we think we do, but we don't. Because God not only knows everything we say, he also knows everything we think!

Take this tape recorder, for example. When you want to say something and to keep a record of it, you can plug the recorder in and get every word just like you said it. Then, if you don't like it or if you don't want it any more, you can do this (erase tape) and the tape is just as if you had never said it. (Play the tape back so that the children can see that the recording is gone.) We think sometimes that this is the way it is in real life, but it's not. Nothing that we ever say can ever be taken back! Once it is said, it is said forever!

Not only do we hurt others when we tell lies, but we hurt ourselves. People get so they won't trust us and even when we say something that *is* true, they won't believe it. Everything you say goes on and on forever; you can never take it back or change it.

Boys and girls who love Jesus want to please Him, and it pleases Jesus when we are honest.

Application Story:

Margo Makes A Decision

Margo jingled the change in her pocket. She took it out and counted it. There was quite a bit left over this afternoon—two nickles and a quarter. "How much shall I take this time," she thought.

Every afternoon after school Margo ran errands for Mrs. Wilson, the little old lady who lived next door to her. Sometimes Margo went to the grocery store, sometimes it was to the drug store, and sometimes it was to the cleaners. Nearly every day old Mrs. Wilson would wave to Margo and beckon for her to come over.

"Would you go to the grocery store for me today, Margo?" Mrs. Wilson had asked this afternoon. "I need a bottle of milk and a loaf of bread."

Margo had left her books at her own house and had run over for the dollar bill Mrs. Wilson was holding out to her. Now she was on her way back to Mrs. Wilson's, the brown bag with the milk and bread in her left arm. The change from the dollar bill was in her right hand which she was holding in her pocket.

Margo was not honest. She wouldn't like for anybody to tell her that she was a cheat or a thief, but that's exactly what she was. For, you see, she didn't always return all of the change to Mrs. Wilson. Like today, she took one of the nickles and put it in her other pocket, leaving only thirty cents to return. It's a good thing Mrs. Wilson can't see too well or she'd catch on, Margo thought.

Sometimes Mrs. Wilson gave something to Margo for running the errands, and sometimes she didn't. This afternoon she gave her a nickle and a cookie. "Thank you, Margo, for helping me," she said as she sat down on the rocker on the front porch. "It sure does get to be a problem when you're old and can't see well. I'm mighty lucky to have a little girl like you living next door to me."

"Thank you," Margo called back to Mrs. Wilson as she went next door to her own house. "I'll see you tomorrow."

That night Margo was working on her problems in arithmetic. One problem was very hard and she couldn't work it. She called her friend, Eleanor, on the phone. "Hi, Eleanor?" she said when Eleanor answered. "What's the answer to the third problem? . . . Okay. . . . Thanks a lot. See you tomorrow at school."

She always called Eleanor when she got stuck on her homework. After she hung up, Margo thought, I'm lucky Eleanor is so smart and will tell me the answers on the phone. It saves a lot of work figuring out how to work these old problems. It's pretty neat sitting next to her in class, too, so I can see the answers on her paper during a test.

The next morning when Margo left for school, she met Jill at the corner. "Hi, Jill," she greeted her friend. "Did you get all your homework by yourself?"

"Well, daddy helped me some," Jill answered. "How about you?"

"I didn't need any help," Margo said. "Those problems were easy."

This was Friday, and after school Margo went out to play with the neighborhood children. They were playing Hide and Seek and when it came her turn to be "It," Margo leaned up against the big tree in her front yard, pretending to close her eyes. Actually, she was peeking and could see where everybody was hiding.

"Five, ten, fifteen, twenty, twenty-five," she started counting, and everybody scattered. ". . . Ninety-five, one hundred! Here I come! Ready or not!" she yelled.

Very casually she went toward where she had seen Jill run. Spying her, she dashed back to home base. "Jill's out!" she called.

That evening after supper, Rev. Swanson came to see Margo and the rest of her family. They had visited a while, and then Mr. Swanson had said, "I wonder if it would be all right for me to talk alone with Margo, Mrs. Worth?"

"Why, yes, surely," Margo's mother answered. "The rest of us will go into the kitchen. Take your time, Pastor. You can call us when you're through."

Margo couldn't imagine what the preacher wanted to see her about. It sort of scared her. When they were alone, Rev. Swanson turned to her and smiled. "I know you're wondering what I want to see you about. It's just that I've not had an opportunity to talk with you about becoming a Christian, Margo, and I think you're old enough now to understand all that Jesus has done for you."

Margo's big hazel eyes looked into Mr. Swanson's blue ones! "I go to Sunday School every Sunday," she said.

"Yes, I know that, Margo. But do you really understand how much Jesus loves you? Do you know He gave His life so you could be saved and be with God forever?"

"Sure, I've heard that."

"Do you think that you need a Savior, Margo?"

"Well, I don't know."

"Do you ever do anything that is wrong? If you do, you are not fit for God to look upon you, because He is perfect and holy."

Margo began to think. Did she ever do anything wrong? Well, she had to admit that she did, sometimes. As a matter of fact, she did pretty often!

She remembered how she stole change from little old Mrs. Wilson and how she lied to Jill and cheated off Eleanor's papers. She knew it was really wrong to peek when she was playing Hide and Seek with the others, too.

The more she thought about it, the more she realized what a bad little girl she really was.

"What can I do, Mr. Swanson?" she asked. "I guess I never really thought about it before, but I do some things that are not right. Does that mean that God doesn't love me?"

"Why, no, Margo. It means just the opposite. God knows you are a sinner and that you do bad things, but He loves you anyway. In fact, He loved you enough to give His Son to die on the cross for you. But you must be sorry for your sins enough to turn away from them and ask God to forgive you. Then you can accept Jesus as your Savior."

"What do I have to do?" Margo wondered.

"Just tell Him that you believe Him and that you want Him to save you, and ask Him to forgive you," Rev. Swanson answered. "We can pray right now if you want to. I'll help you. You can repeat your prayer after me."

The preacher and Margo bowed their heads and closed their eyes. Margo repeated after Mr. Swanson: "Dear God, Thank You for loving me enough to give Jesus for me. I accept Him as my Savior. I am sorry for all the things I have done wrong and with Your help I will turn away from them. Please forgive me and let Jesus come into my heart. In Jesus' Name. Amen."

There was a happy smile on Margo's face when she lifted her head. She jumped up and ran into the kitchen to get her parents. "Mom! Dad! I've just let Jesus come into my heart!" she said. They both put their arms around her and gave her a big squeeze. She knew that they were happy for her decision.

After Rev. Swanson left, Margo went to her room to do some thinking. She was thinking about sin and all of the things she had done wrong. She went to her drawer where she kept her piggy bank. Now that I'm a Christian, the first thing I'm going to do is ask Mrs. Wilson to forgive me. I'll give her back all of her money, too. I'm glad I didn't spend it! I'm going to stop cheating on my homework and on tests at school, too. I'll stop cheating when I play games, too. God must love me an awfully lot to forgive me of all the bad things I've done. I'm going to show Him how much I love Him by being a better girl. I'm glad Rev. Swanson came to see me. I feel like a new person!

Margo was right. She was a new person. Not on the outside, where other people could see, but on the inside, where God can see!

Bible Story:

The Baptism Of Jesus

John the Baptist was a strange man. At least, we would consider him strange if we saw him today.

His clothes were made out of camels' hair and he wore a leather belt around his waist.

John had been living in the wilderness for a long time and because he couldn't buy food and didn't grow it, he ate locusts and wild honey.

One day, God told John to come out of the wilderness and preach to the people and baptize them when they realized that they were sinners and repented of their sins.

John the Baptist preached and preached. People came from the big city of Jerusalem and all over Judea to hear him as he preached beside the Jordan River. When the people acknowledged that they were sinners and were sorry for their sins, he baptized them right there in the river.

John was a brave man because he told the people right to their faces what bad people they were.

"Repent!" he shouted. "Repent! Be baptized! Live a good life showing that you really are sorry for being such a bad sinner. Let people see the change in you. Share what you own. If you have two coats, give one of them to someone who doesn't have a coat at all. If you have some food, share it with someone who is hungry!"

To the tax collectors, he said, "Be honest and don't take anything that doesn't belong to you."

To the soldiers, he said, "Be gentle and don't lie about anything. Be content with what you have and don't take anything from anyone else."

John preached and preached. Then, when somebody would repent as he told them to, they would wade out into the river and John baptized them right there.

John said, "I baptize you with water unto repentance, but someone is coming who is greater by far than I ever was. I'm not even good enough to tie his shoe strings. When He comes He will baptize you with the Holy Spirit. No one has ever seen God except this man, Jesus Christ."

One day while John was at the River Jordan preaching and baptizing, he saw Jesus coming toward him. He said, "Behold, this is the Lamb of God which taketh away the sin of the world."

Jesus walked up to John and asked John to baptize Him.

"What? You want me to baptize You?" John exclaimed. "Why, I should be the one asking You to baptize *me!* I'm not worthy to baptize you!"

Jesus answered, "But this is right. I want you to baptize me."

John reluctantly waded out into the river. Jesus followed him. Both of them bowed their heads and prayed.

John gently lowered Jesus into the water until He was completely covered. Then he lifted Jesus up so that He was standing upright again in the water.

Everyone on the shore was quiet as they watched John baptize Jesus. They knew that something very unusual was happening.

Just then, the heavens opened up and a beautiful white dove flew down out of the sky and lighted on Jesus' shoulder. Then there was a rumbling sound and God's voice came from heaven. He said, "This is my beloved Son in whom I am well pleased."

John knew for sure now that this was really Jesus Christ, the Son of God. He had heard God Himself say so!

PROGRAM 7
GOD CAN USE US

Larger Scripture Lesson: Acts 1:1-12; Matthew 28:16-20

Scripture for Children's Church: Matthew 28:16-20

Object Lesson:

God Needs Us!

Object: A globe

When the astronauts were out in space, they looked back at the world and this is what it looked like to them! (Point out globe.) It was round like a ball. They could see where the oceans were and they could see each distinct continent.

They saw North America and South America. They saw Europe and Africa and Asia. They saw Australia. (Point each one of these out.) It must have seemed strange to them to know that all of the people they knew and loved were so far away.

Even if the astronauts had super, super vision and had been able to see the people on the continents at which they were looking, they couldn't have seen the people on the other side of the world. (Illustrate by using globe.) When they were looking at the United States, they couldn't see the people in China. When they were looking at China, they wouldn't have been able to see the people in the United States.

But God can see everybody all of the time! He not only can see us all of the time, but He knows what each one of us is thinking! He can do this because He is a Spirit.

In spite of the fact that God can do all of this, He still needs us! He needs us to tell other people about Him. If people don't know God and if they don't read their Bibles, they don't have any way of learning about Him, except through someone like you and me.

When Jesus went to heaven, He gave what is called the "Great Commission" to His disciples. He told them to go to people and teach them about Him and baptize them in the Name of the

Father and of the Son and of the Holy Spirit.

We are His disciples, so we should tell people about Jesus, too.

Application Story:

Jane Becomes A Missionary

Jane kept looking straight at Miss Weeks. She listened very carefully to everything Miss Weeks said. Oh, what a wonderful thing it must be to be a missionary, Jane thought. That's what I want to be when I grow up.

"Being a missionary to Africa is not a very easy job, but it is very interesting," Miss Weeks was saying. "The Lord has blessed me even when I was sick."

"One time I got very sick," she continued. "A little girl found me lying on a path in the jungle where I had fainted. The little girl and her mother nursed me back to health. I could have gone to live with other missionaries, but I felt like this was a wonderful opportunity God had given me to live in this home. They didn't know about Jesus, but they were very kind. I'm so happy to be able to tell you that before I left that little thatch hut, Miri and her mother and her father all had accepted Jesus as their Savior. They were such happy Christians that their whole tribe is now trying to find the peace that they have."

"But you don't have to go to a foreign country to be a missionary," Miss Weeks said. "You can be a missionary wherever you are."

Jane thought of all of the people she knew who didn't know Jesus. She thought of her mother and her father first of all. She thought of her aunts and uncles and cousins. She thought of her friends at school.

After the meeting, Jane inspected all of the ivory carvings that Miss Weeks had on display. They were beautiful. She looked at the photographs of Miss Weeks and the boys and girls with whom she worked. I want to be a missionary some day, Jane thought again. She was pleased when Miss Weeks smiled at her as she left the church to go home.

That night while Jane was sleeping, she became very ill. By morning she had a high fever and her mother called the doctor.

"Jane has a severe infection," the doctor explained to her mother. "She must stay in bed and be very quiet."

Jane was too sick to be anything else but quiet for several days.

But when she began to feel better, she began to fuss because she didn't want to stay in bed.

Then she remembered how Miss Weeks had been sick and how God had blessed her because of it. Maybe there's a reason for my being sick, too, Jane thought. If God wants to use me like He used Miss Weeks, I had better act nicer than this!

Two of Jane's friends came to see her after school one afternoon. "When I get well I'd like for you to go to Sunday School with me," Jane said.

"Okay," Mary answered. "I've been wondering if it would be all right for me to go!"

"I'll ask my mother if I can go, too," Louise said.

Jane's mother was in the room with the girls. "I just might go along with you!" she said.

"Oh, Mother! Really? If you will, I'll be so glad!"

"Well, I don't see why I can't," Mother answered.

That night, when Jane's father came home, she asked him if he'd go to Sunday School, too.

"Well, if Mother goes, I might," he said as he pinched Jane's big toe sticking up under the blanket.

"Miss Weeks said we don't have to go any place to be a missionary. I know what she meant now," Jane said. "And some day I might get to go to another country, too. But I'd better practice right here until then. I can see why I got sick now. God could use me better that way. He had something He wanted me to do and that was the way He helped me to do it."
Bible Story:

The Great Commission

After Jesus died on the cross, He rose again. He didn't stay dead like an ordinary person, because He *wasn't* an ordinary person! Jesus was a man, but He was God, too!

When Jesus arose from the grave, He stayed on earth for forty days. Then it was time for Him to leave the earth and go to stay in heaven.

Just before He left the earth, He and His eleven disciples met in Galilee on a mountain called Olivet. While they were there together, Jesus reminded them of all of the things He had taught them.

"I want you to be missionaries," He said. "I want you to go out into your own city and out into the state and into the other states. I want you to even go to other countries!"

"And when you go," He said, "I want you to teach the people about Me. When they have accepted Me as their Savior, I want you to baptize them in the name of the Father, and the Son, and of the Holy Spirit."

"Teach them all of the things I have taught you," He said. "If you will do these things, I will always be with you."

Then Jesus put His hands up over His head to bless the disciples. Slowly He began to rise. He went up, up until they could no longer see Him.

The disciples just stood there, looking at where Jesus had been. Their eyes were opened wide and their heads were turned toward the sky.

Suddenly, there were two angels standing beside them.

"Why are you gazing up at the sky?" one of the angels said. "Jesus will come back. He'll come back in the same way He left."

The disciples turned and walked back toward Jerusalem. While they were walking, they thought about all of the wonderful things they had seen Jesus do. They thought about what Jesus had told them they should do. They promised themselves that they would do all of the things that Jesus had told them to do.

"Teach others about Me, and I will be with you," Jesus had said. And what He told His disciples then was intended for us, too.

"He said, "Go to the people who live in your own city and tell them about me. Go to all the people in your state and in your country. Go to all the people of the world."

Jesus wants us all to be missionaries.

PROGRAM 8
WE BELONG TO GOD

Larger Scripture Lesson: Acts 16:13-15

Scripture for Children's Church: Acts 16:13-15

Object Lesson:

Everything Has Its Purpose

Object: Matches

Everything has its purpose. And usually, when we use something for a wrong purpose, it doesn't turn out right.

For instance, your shoe is made to wear on your foot. If you tried to use it for a glove, it wouldn't fit and it just wouldn't work!

Vitamin pills are supposed to make you healthy. But you are only supposed to take one or two a day. If you tried to use them for candy, you'd find that they not only don't taste good, but they would make you sick!

A rolling pin is made to roll out dough, not to stir it.

A washing machine is made to wash clothes, not dry them.

And then there are matches. (Show matches) They are very useful—when used for the right purpose. You can use them to light a fire in the fireplace, or to light a burner on a gas stove. But you are not supposed to use them to light big fires that burn down people's houses. You are not supposed to use them to cause forest fires. And I don't believe you are supposed to use them to light cigarettes.

Our bodies are the temples of God. We don't know what good cigarettes are, but we have heard a lot about the bad things they can do to our bodies.

We must always be careful to use everything for the purpose for which God intends it. We should remember that our bodies are temples of God and we should use them to show others about Him.

Application Story:

A Different Kind Of Funeral

"When we accept Jesus as our Savior, He comes into our hearts. And since He is in our hearts, our bodies become His home. We should always remember that our bodies are temples of God. When we remember that, it isn't so hard for us to take care of them properly.

"If our bodies are temples of God, we should want to keep them in good repair. How do we do that? Can you tell me one way, Glenn?"

Glenn jumped. He had been listening to Mr. Ord, his Sunday School teacher, but now that Mr. Ord had called on him, his mind went sort of blank.

"Perhaps you can tell me, Jeff?" Mr. Ord asked.

"Well, we can eat right and we can get plenty of sleep. Is that what you mean?"

"Yes, that's very good, Jeff. Now can you think of something else we can do, Glenn?"

Glenn fidgeted in his chair. He didn't like being put on the spot like this.

"Well, Wiley, can you tell us some more things we can do to protect our bodies as temples of God?"

"We can take good care of them when it's cold or rainy so we don't get sick," Wiley answered. "And we can take vitamins, too, can't we?"

"Fine, Wiley. Let's see. We have said that we can eat properly and get plenty of sleep. We can keep our bodies warm when it's cold and cool when it's hot. We can be careful not to do things that will make us sick. We can take vitamins. Does anybody else have anything to add?"

Glenn cleared his throat. "We can be careful and not put anything in them that is harmful. Like beer or whiskey or cigarette smoke."

"You are right, Glenn. I'm so glad you said that, because it is often a temptation to do things we shouldn't do. I hope that we can remember to use our bodies for God and always have them clean for Him."

The closing bell rang and Mr. Ord dismissed his class. The boys quickly scattered and soon Glenn and his best chum, Jeff, were alone walking toward the church auditorium and to their seats. Glenn didn't have much to say. He was thinking about their Sunday School lesson. He'd never thought much about the things Mr. Ord had talked about today.

The bulge in his left back pocket seemed bigger than ever now. He cautiously checked to see if the flap was still fastened. He hoped nobody'd ask him what was in there.

Church was finally over. Glenn and Jeff left together.

"What's the matter, Glenn?" Jeff asked. "Don't you feel good?"

"Oh, I feel all right, I guess," Glenn answered.

"Well, something's wrong. What is it?" Jeff insisted.

"Oh, nothing," Glenn mumbled. "Nothing at all."

After the two boys had walked a little farther, Glenn spoke again. "I thought I had something keen, but I don't know now. Look!"

He pulled out what was making the bulge in his pocket. It was a little package. Carefully he unwrapped the kleenex around it. It was a book of matches and two cigarettes.

"Uncle Frank was over at our house last night, and he gave me these. I thought we could go out behind the garage and smoke them today. But now I'm not so sure that I want to. What do you think?"

"Well, I know they aren't good for you. But some people act like they think smoking is pretty swell. Why don't we try it?"

"I don't know. Mr. Ord said that our bodies are temples of God if we are Christians, and we're both Christians."

"Oh, come on. I know lots of people who are Christians that smoke."

"That doesn't make it right, though," Glenn argued.

"Well, give them to me if you don't want them," Jeff said.

"No, because then I'd be causing you to do wrong. No, I just think I'll throw them away."

"Oh, no you don't," Jeff shouted as he grabbed the cigarettes and matches. "Thanks," he yelled, running off toward his house.

"Oh, no you don't," Glenn yelled back as he chased Jeff. "Give that back!"

Just as Jeff reached his front walk Glenn caught up with him.

Jeff said as he handed the package back to his friend, "I don't want them anyway. I just wanted to see what you'd do."

"Thanks," Glenn said. "See you later."

Walking on toward home, he thought, "These things are already causing me trouble."

His mother and father had reached home before he had. He heard them talking in the living room. "Isn't it too bad about Mr. Haney?" he heard his mother say. "The doctors say he has lung cancer."

"I know Mr. Haney," Glenn thought, remembering how often he

had seen Mr. Haney with a cigarette hanging out of his mouth. "Well, that settles it for me!"

After dinner, Glenn excused himself from the table and went down to the basement to get a shovel. Then he took the shovel out into the back yard. He started to dig. It won't take too wide a hole, he thought, but I'm going to make it deep. When he had finished digging, he pulled the troublesome package from his pocket.

Just then Jeff came around to the back of the house.

"Hi! What're you doing?" he called.

"Just having a little funeral. I'm burying these matches and cigarettes. And, as far as I'm concerned, it's the funeral for all cigarettes for me. Mr. Ord said to remember that our bodies are temples of God. And I'm not going to pollute my body with these old things. I'm going to bury them so they won't have a chance to bury me! I want to keep my body healthy and clean so Jesus can use it."

"Yeah, you're right," Jeff agreed. "Here, let me help."

Bible Story:

Lydia Serves God

Lydia lived in the City of Thyratira. She was a business woman who sold purple dye. This was unusual at the time she was living because women usually stayed at home. Evidently there was no man to take care of Lydia, so she had to work. She must have been a good business woman, too, because she had a large house and many servants.

Every Saturday, which was their day of rest, Lydia met with some of her friends down by the river, where they sat in the shade of the big trees and watched the clear green water flow down into the valley. It was a beautiful place to worship God. Here they prayed, sang songs, and read some of the Old Testament together.

Lydia and her friends had not heard about Jesus yet, because He had lived and died and risen again far away from them. He had lived in Asia and these ladies lived in Europe. They didn't have newspapers, airplanes, television sets, or radios, like we have today to bring them news from faraway countries. They had to wait until a traveler told them what was going on in the rest of the world.

One Sabbath Day while Lydia and her friends were praying and singing by the river, they saw three men approaching.

"Won't you join us?" Lydia invited. She wanted everyone to feel welcome to their worship services.

"Thank you very much," one of the men answered. "My name is Paul, and these men are my friends, Luke and Silas. Are you having a worship service?"

"Yes, we are," Lydia answered. "I am Lydia and these ladies are my friends. Would you like to speak to us?"

"I would consider it a great privilege," Paul said. "We have been directed to come here by God. When we were in Troas we were planning on preaching some more in Asia, but God gave me a vision. In this vision I saw a man with outstretched arms. 'Come over to Macedonia and help us,' the man cried. We immediately came over to Macedonia, as God directed. We are telling everyone about Jesus as we travel."

"Who is this Jesus?" Lydia and the other women asked.

"He is the Son of God whom God had promised to send to save us from our sins," Paul answered.

"We have been looking for the Savior. Do you mean He has already come? Tell us about Him," Lydia urged.

"Yes, tell us about Him," the other ladies repeated.

"Well, several years ago—in fact, about the time I myself was born—there was a virgin whose name was Mary. An angel came to her and told her that she was going to have a baby. 'This baby will be God's Son,' the angel said, 'and you are to call Him Jesus.' "

Paul told the ladies all about how Jesus had been born and how He had grown up and how He had told the people that they could become members of the kingdom of God. He told them, too, about how all of the people had not accepted Jesus, but some of them had killed Him by nailing Him to a cross.

"But," Paul said, "that was not the end of Jesus. He didn't stay dead! On the third day He rose again, just as He had said He would do. And now He is in heaven with God."

"What a wonderful story," Lydia sighed.

"Oh, it's not just a story," Paul said. "It's a fact. And it's a fact, too, that anyone who is sorry he is a sinner and asks God to forgive Him can have Jesus as his Savior and have eternal life!"

Lydia looked thoughtfully at Paul. "Do you mean that if I accept Jesus as my Savior I will have eternal life?"

"Yes," Paul answered, "that's what I mean."

"I do accept Him," Lydia said.

Paul then told her that she should be baptized to prove her love for God.

"Can you baptize me?" Lydia asked.

Many of the other women nodded their heads. This Jesus must have been the Savior for whom they were looking.

Paul was happy to baptize Lydia and the other women who accepted Jesus as their Savior. He did it right there in the beautiful river near where they had been worshiping.

Lydia was glad that Paul and his friends had come to Thyratira so they could learn about Jesus.

"It would be good if you could stay here for a while," she said. "We have many things to learn. Then all of my household and all of my other friends can learn about Jesus, too. I'd be very happy if you would stay at my house."

Paul was grateful for Lydia's invitation, and he and Luke and Silas went home with her. She made nice beds for them and saw that they got plenty of good food. She took care of them all of the time they stayed in Thyratira. She knew that she was serving God by looking after His servants.

Lydia wanted to use everything she had for Jesus.

PROGRAM 9
BAPTISM

Larger Scripture Lesson: Acts 8:26-40

Scripture for Children's Church: Acts 8:35-37

Object Lesson:

Water Has Many Uses

Object: A glass of water

Water is very important in our lives. In fact, without water we couldn't even live!

You've heard people say, "We sure need a good rain!" That's because plants and trees and grass need to be watered or they shrivel up and die. And when our plants die—plants like potatoes and peas and corn and carrots—we don't have any vegetables to eat.

If we don't get rain, fruit doesn't grow well, either. It is little and doesn't taste very good.

But do you know that water is more important to our bodies than vegetables or fruit? If we didn't have any water to drink, we would die of thirst!

We use water to wash, too. Just think how dirty we would get if we never washed!

God tells us in the Bible that water is used for something else, too. And that is for baptizing people.

Before we become Christians we are all dirty with sin. But when we ask God to forgive us of our sins and ask Jesus to be our Saviour, those sins are all taken away and we become clean in God's sight.

God wants us to be baptized after we have accepted Jesus as our Savior. Baptism is to show others that we are Christians. When we are baptized, we are lowered into the water and raised up out of it again. This is like a picture showing that we were dirty with sin. As we go down into the water and come up, our

46

sins are washed away by Jesus. We rise up, clean and new.

We don't have to be baptized to be Christians, but if we love Jesus and want to obey Him, we will be baptized because we know that is what He wants us to do.

Application Story:

Trudy Gets Baptized

Trudy was excited! She was going to be baptized!

Right now she was waiting in the room beside the baptistry. Dressed in a white robe which almost reached her ankles, she was waiting for Reverend Davenport, who was standing in the center, to call her out into the water.

Trudy had accepted Jesus as her Savior several Sundays ago when her Sunday School teacher had come to visit her in her home. Mrs. Williams had told her all about how Jesus had died for her sins, and how He had risen again and had overcome death. She had asked Trudy if she would like to let Jesus be her Savior.

"If you would," Mrs. Williams said, "we'll pray right now and ask Him to come into your heart."

"I'd like that," Trudy answered, "because I love Jesus."

Mrs. Williams and Trudy both bowed their heads and talked to God. Mrs. Williams helped Trudy put into words what was in her heart. Her prayer had been something like this: "Dear God, I know I have done many things that have displeased you and I am sorry. I love Jesus and want to be like Him. I want to let Him come into my heart right now. Thank You. Amen."

Trudy and Mrs. Williams raised their heads. Trudy's eyes were shining.

"Why, that's very easy," Mrs. Williams said. "All you have to do is ask God to help you to know what He wants you to do and read the Bible. Soon you'll know the Bible so well that you'll begin to know His will almost automatically. Anyway, you'll begin to recognize it and wait for it. Here, let me show you."

Mrs. Williams leafed through Trudy's Bible. "Look here in Matthew *3:16* and *17*. We find John the Baptist baptizing people in the River Jordan. Jesus came up to him and said, 'I want you to baptize Me, too, John.' Well, John thought Jesus didn't need to be baptized because He was God's Son and He had never done anything wrong. But Jesus insisted. So, John took Him out into the river and lowered Him back into the water until He was completely covered. Then John knew for sure that he had done the right thing because when Jesus came up out of the water 'the heavens were opened unto him, and he saw the Spirit of God descending like a dove, and lighting upon Him. And, lo, a voice from heaven, saying, 'This is my beloved Son, in whom I am well pleased.' "

Mrs. Williams continued. "Trudy, *if* it was important to Jesus to be baptized, we know it is important for us to be baptized, too. Don't we?"

"Yes, I guess so," Trudy answered. "But why is it so important?"

Mrs. Williams took Trudy's hand and held it in her own. Trudy could tell that Mrs. Williams loved her very much. She listened carefully as her teacher answered her question.

"I think it is important to God because it proves something. It proves that we really love Jesus. It's something we can do right after we accept Him as our Savior. If we are baptized we are telling the whole world that we love Jesus. And that's what we are supposed to do."

Mrs. Williams continued, "You see, Trudy, *baptism is like a picture of salvation.* When a person goes under the water it shows that he has given himself to Jesus. Then, while he is under the water, it is a picture of his sins being washed away. When he comes up out of the water, it shows him a new, clean person who belongs to God. Here, Trudy, read this."

Mrs. Williams pointed to a verse in the Book of Romans.

Trudy took the Bible and read out loud. "Therefore, we are buried with him by baptism unto death, that as Christ was raised up from the dead by the glory of the Father, even so we also should walk in newness of life" (Romans 6:4).

Trudy scratched her head. "I guess this verse means that when we are baptized, we are following Jesus and showing others that we believe Jesus rose after He died. Then we need to act like Christians. Is that right?"

"Yes. That's very good. I know the Bible is hard to understand for many people, but now that you are a Christian you'll be able to understand it better. If you read it every day it will become easier and easier. And we'll keep on studying it in Sunday School, too. You can always ask me or Reverend Davenport if you have any questions or if you don't understand something. Then some day you'll be able to help people understand it yourself!"

"Can I get baptized, Mrs. Williams?"

"Why, sure, Trudy. I'm sure you've seen many baptismal services in our church. All you have to do is to go up in front of the church during the last song in a worship service and tell Reverend Davenport that you love Jesus and want to be baptized. Then he'll tell you when our next baptismal service will be. Would you like to do that Sunday?"

"Yes," Trudy answered. "I want everyone to know that I love Jesus, and the sooner the better."

"That's fine. But you don't have to wait that long to tell others that you love Jesus. You should start telling people right away. Let's tell your mother right now. She won't mind coming in from the kitchen to hear this good news! And tell your friends at school, too. The more people you tell, the more will be won to Jesus through you. You see, you are Christ's ambassador now. That means that you'll always represent Jesus, no matter where you are."

Trudy jumped up from the divan. "Mother, Mother," she called as she hurried to the kitchen. "I just let Jesus come into my heart. Is it all right if I get baptized?"

Trudy's mother came out of the kitchen, meeting her daughter. "Oh, Trudy" she said, "I'm so happy for you! Of course it's all right!"

All of this had taken place two weeks ago. Now Trudy was standing just outside the baptistry waiting to be called into the water by Reverend Davenport.

She looked at the pretty painted picture behind the water. It was supposed to look like the River Jordan where Jesus was baptized. She looked down at the white robe the church had furnished her. It made her feel very special. "I am very special to Jesus," she thought.

Reverend Davenport beckoned to her and reached out to help her down the steps. The water was warm and came up almost to her shoulders, but she felt safe holding Reverend Davenport's hand. She looked out into the auditorium. She couldn't see anybody because it was dark out there. But she knew that her mother and her father and Mrs. Williams and lots of others that she knew were watching. She followed Reverend Davenport to the center of the baptistry and listened as he spoke.

Then, slowly he lowered her down into the water until it was over her head. "Oh, Jesus," she thought, "thank You for loving me so much."

Trudy pushed her streaming wet hair out of her face when she felt the bottom of the tank with her feet. She walked back up the baptistry steps. She was glad she had obeyed God and had been baptized like Jesus.

Bible Story:

Philip And The Ethiopian

Philip loved God. He loved God's Son, Jesus, too. In fact, Philip loved God and Jesus so much that he wanted to let everybody know how great and wonderful they were!

Somebody gave Philip a nickname. It was "Philip the Evangelist." An evangelist is someone who travels around preaching about Jesus.

We have evangelists today, too. They are men who come to our church for special services and stay several weeks at a time. We call these meetings Revivals. The men preach every night during the week, and people bring their friends so they can hear about Jesus.

One day Philip was praying. "Dear God," he said, "please show me somebody that I can talk to about Jesus."

While he was thinking about God and praying, an angel spoke to him. Philip listened very carefully because he knew that God had sent the angel. This is what the angel said: "Get up, Philip, and leave Jerusalem. Take the road that goes south toward Gaza."

Philip didn't waste any time. He jumped up and started on his way. While he was walking along, he saw a beautiful carriage being pulled by a sleek black horse. He knew that whoever was riding in that chariot must be very rich and important. He looked more closely. There was a black man inside. "He must be returning to his home in Ethiopia which is in Africa," Philip thought. "He looked like he was reading something. What was it? It must be something he had bought in Jerusalem. It must be very interesting, too, because he isn't paying any attention to where the carriage is going or to the scenery he is passing. He just keeps his eyes on the scroll he's reading. He must be reading out loud, too, because his lips are moving."

While Philip was thinking about all these things, God spoke to him. "Go up and join the man in the chariot," He said.

Philip ran up to the chariot. He listened to the man. He was reading from the Bible! He was reading from the Book of Isaiah!

"Do you understand what you are reading?" Philip asked the man.

"How can I? It's so hard," the man answered. "I need someone to teach me. Can you help me?"

"Yes," Philip answered.

"Good," the man said. "Climb up here and sit beside me."

Philip climbed up into the fancy chariot and sat beside the man.

"Here," said the man. "What does this mean? 'He was led as a sheep to the slaughter; and like a lamb dumb before his shearer, so opened he not his mouth; In his humiliation his judgment was taken away, and who shall declare his generation? For his life is taken from the earth.' "

"Who is the prophet Isaiah talking about here?" the Ethiopian asked. "Himself or some other man?"

"Isaiah was talking about Jesus, the Son of God," Philip answered. "Even though Isaiah lived at least 700 years before Jesus was born, God told Isaiah all about Jesus. God told him to write all these things down so the Hebrew people could have hope in God's promise that He was going to send a Savior who would take away the sins of the world. Jesus is the One that you may have heard about while you were in Jerusalem. He was the One God promised to send. He was killed by the Jews not too long ago. He allowed them to nail Him to a cross to die. He was the lamb being led to the slaughter that Isaiah spoke of. He didn't protest because He knew it was God's will. He had to die so we can have eternal life. When they took Him off of the cross, they laid his dead body in a tomb. But do you know what happened? He didn't stay dead! Because He was God's Son and had never sinned in His whole life, He could overcome death! When His friends went back to visit Him in His tomb to put spices and ointment on His body, the body wasn't there! Only His grave clothes were in the tomb, just exactly where His body had been lying!

"After that, Jesus came in His new resurrected body to see His disciples. He talked with them and ate with them. He was seen by many other people, too. He was even seen by 500 people at the same time! Most of them are still alive.

"Anyone who realizes that he is a sinner and that he falls short of the wonderful glory of God, can accept Jesus as his Savior if he is sorry for his sins and tells God so. Then he can have eternal life with God, just like Jesus. When people accept Him as their Savior they can be baptized to show others that they are now followers of Jesus. Jesus Himself was baptized while He was living on earth. He walked out into the River Jordan and John the Baptist took Him and lowered Him back into the water.

"Baptism is like a picture," Philip told the Ethiopian. "It shows a person as a sinner before he goes under the water. Then while he is under, it is a picture of the washing away of his sins. When he comes up out of the water, he is the picture of a new man, cleansed from his sins."

Philip and the Ethiopian had been riding along as they talked. The Ethiopian listened to every word Philip said. He kept nodding his head. He was very glad Philip had come when he did.

Just then they were passing a small lake.

"Look! There's some water! What keeps me from being baptized right now?" the man asked Philip.

"Nothing at all, if you believe with all of your heart all of the things I've just told you," Philip answered.

"I do. I do," the man said. "I believe that Jesus Christ is the Son of God."

"Then let's go down to the lake."

"Stop the chariot," the black man called to his driver, "and wait here."

Philip and the man climbed out of the chariot and walked down to the little lake. They walked out into the water until it was almost up to their waists. Here they stopped, and Philip lowered the man down until even his head was under the water. Then he lifted him up. The Ethiopian was dripping wet, but he was very happy. Philip didn't mind being wet either, because it was warm, and because he was glad the Ethiopian had accepted Jesus as his Savior.

The two men walked out of the lake back toward the chariot.

Suddenly, the Ethiopian was all alone. The Spirit of God had caught Philip away and set him down in the City of Azotus!

Now Philip continued to tell everyone about Jesus, just as he had done before. He was happy because he knew that he was doing what God wanted him to do.

The Ethiopian was happy, too! Now that he had learned about Jesus he was going to go back to his own country and tell all the people about Him! Now he would become an evangelist, just like Philip!

PROGRAM 10
FOLLOWING GOD

Larger Scripture Lesson: Numbers 22-24

Scripture for Children's Church: Numbers 22:7-12

Object Lesson:

A Change For The Best

Object: Needle, thread, button

Some time ago, this button came off of my coat, and I put it in my pocket so I wouldn't lose it. Now, the button doesn't do any good in my pocket because it is not doing the job for which it was made. The coat isn't doing its best at the job for which it was made, either. When it is cold and the wind is blowing, I get cold because the coat doesn't keep me as warm as it's supposed to!

However, if I take this needle and thread and use them for the purpose for which they were made and sew the button back where it belongs, there certainly is a change for the best.

People are like buttons. Unless we do what we are supposed to do, we aren't of too much value. The button in my pocket doesn't do any good at all. If you don't do what God wants you to do, then you aren't really much good. Neither am I. If we let God help us and if we read our Bibles, we can change, just like this button did when it was sewn on my coat.

Application Story:

Johnny Learns A Lesson

Johnny Greenlease was a grumpy boy. He grumbled about everybody and everything. If somebody *didn't* do something for him, he grumbled. If somebody *did* do something for him, he grumbled. If a dog was brown, he liked black better; if the dog was black, he liked brown. If somebody gave him something, he always thought that they wanted something in return. Anyway, he never liked it.

It's a wonder Johnny had any friends at all, but he did. He had one very good friend whose name was Richard Martin. Richard was just the opposite of Johnny. Richard was happy and he appreciated everything anybody did for him. He never argued about anything, and he smiled a lot and was kind to everyone. Richard loved people, and people knew that he loved them by the way he acted.

Sometimes Johnny was unkind to Richard, but Richard was always nice to Johnny.

One day, Johnny and Richard were walking home from school. They took a shortcut through the park and Johnny stopped to climb a tree.

"Come on up!" he called.

"I can't. I'll ruin my pants," Richard called back.

"Oh, come on. You can be careful."

"No, I'd better not."

"Come on. Be a sport."

So, Richard climbed up into the tree and joined Johnny on the branch. The branch looked strong and healthy, but, without any warning at all, there was a loud crack, and the branch and the two boys were falling to the hard ground below.

Crash! The sound of the splintering branch almost drowned out Johnny's yell. "Ow!" But Richard was strangely silent. When the dust settled and the noise subsided, Johnny called out, "Hey, Rich! Are you all right?"

Richard didn't answer. He lay quiet and still.

"Rich! Rich!"

Johnny crawled over to his friend. Richard's pale face was streaked with blood flowing from a gash in his forehead. Johnny was scared. He tried to get Rich out from under the branch, but it was too big and heavy. He looked toward the left and toward the right. There was no one in sight.

"Rich! Rich!"

Johnny took a clean handkerchief from his pocket and placed it on the cut. He had heard that pressure stopped bleeding. He hoped it worked. Seconds later, Johnny decided he'd better run for help.

"Rich, I'll be right back," he said. "I'm going to get help."

He ran as fast as he could. He knew the people who lived in the house next to the park. He hoped they were home.

"Mrs. Adams! Mrs. Adams! Help!"

Mrs. Adams appeared in her doorway. "Johnny! What's wrong?"

"It's Richard. He's hurt bad. He's under a branch and I can't get him out! His head's cut and he's bleeding, too!"

Mrs. Adams ran back into the house and soon appeared with her husband and son.

"You call an ambulance. We'll go see what we can do," Mr. Adams told his wife as he and his son Bill hurried after Johnny.

Soon a siren's shrill wail pierced the air. Mrs. Adams motioned for the attendants to follow her into the park.

"Over here!" she directed.

Mr. Adams and Bill had helped Johnny lift the branch off Richard. His cut had stopped bleeding and he was conscious, but he lay very quiet, his left leg strangely twisted under him. He didn't complain once. Johnny stood over him, fully aware of the danger into which he had prodded Richard. He felt responsible for Richard's being hurt. Richard was his friend—actually, his only true friend—and he, Johnny had caused him to be lying there quiet and still beside the big branch which they had been sitting on.

Johnny didn't want anyone to see him cry, because he didn't want people to think he was a sissy. After the ambulance had carried Richard away and Johnny had gone home, he lay on his bed, sobs wracking his body at every breath. He felt so sorry for Richard. What could he do to help now?

As soon as he could, he called the hospital on the telephone.

"I'm sorry. We have no report on Richard Martin," said the voice on the other end of the line.

Johnny hung up the receiver. He picked it up again. This time he called Richard's house. No one answered.

"May I go over to the hospital?" he asked his mother. "I want to see how Richie is."

"Yes, I guess you'd better," his mother said. "You'll be a nervous wreck if you don't."

It wasn't far to the hospital, so Johnny walked. While he walked, he thought. "Richard is a really swell guy. He never gripes or grumbles about anything. I sure hope he's not hurt bad. He's too nice a guy to have this happen to him. I'm such a griper that nobody but Richard likes me. It should have happened to me and then nobody'd be worried—well, nobody except maybe Mom and Dad and Richie." The farther he walked, the more he thought. By the time he had reached the long stairway that led up to the hospital entrance, he had made a decision. "I'm going to be more like Richard," he decided. "I'm going to appreciate what I have and quit all my griping and grumping around. I'm going to be a good friend to Richie and everybody else, too."

He climbed the outside stairs and passed through the revolving doors into the hospital lobby. There he saw Mr. Martin, Richard's father. "Hello there," Mr. Martin said. "I was just on my way over to your house to get you. Richard thought you might come over to see him. The doctors are looking him over now, but they seem to think he's in pretty good shape. He may have a broken leg, but they haven't taken x-rays yet. We're grateful it's no worse than it is."

"Boy! I am, too!" Johnny said. "I'm glad that Richie is going to be all right."

"Isn't that something?" Johnny thought to himself. "I'm already changing. I'm glad he's better instead of mad because all this happened. I'm already beginning to look on the good side of things!"

Bible Story:

Balaam's Donkey Talks To Him

Balaam lived a long, long time before Jesus. We read about him in the Old Testament. God didn't speak to everybody during Old Testament times, but He spoke to Balaam. Sometimes Balaam did what God told him to do; sometimes he was careless and didn't pay attention to what God told him.

One time, when the Israelites were fighting the Moabites, the Moabites became very frightened. The Israelites were winning, and the Moabites didn't know what to do.

"We will all be killed!" they cried to their king.

"There is still something we can do," King Balak said. "I will call the prophet Balaam here and tell him to curse these people so we can drive them out of our country."

King Balak sent some important men of the kingdom to Balaam. When the messengers told Balaam what King Balak wanted him to do, he answered, "Stay here tonight. I will talk to God and in the morning I will tell you what He says."

That night God talked to Balaam. "Who are these men who are here with you?" God asked.

"King Balak sent them to me," Balaam answered. "They have told me that the Israelites are fighting the Moabites and King Balak wants me to curse them so the Moabites can win the battle."

"You cannot curse them, because I have already blessed them," God said. "Do not go to King Balak."

The next morning, Balak told the men that God had spoken to him. "Go back home," he said. "God has told me not to go with you."

When the messengers went back to the king without Balaam and told him that Balaam had said he could not come, King Balak said, "I will send more important men than the last ones to Balaam. Perhaps they can convince him to come and curse the Israelites."

When the men were ready to leave, Balak said, "Tell Balaam I will give him great honors if he will come. I'll give him anything he wants."

When the second group of men told Balaam what King Balak had said, he answered, "Tell King Balak that even if he gave me his house full of silver and gold I wouldn't come to curse the Israelites. God has ordered me not to go. I must do what He says, but stay here tonight, and I'll ask God again."

That night God spoke to Balaam again. "I have told you what I want you to do, but go, if you insist," God said.

The next morning Balaam got up and saddled his donkey so he could go with the princes to King Balak.

God was angry because Balaam was going after He had told him not to go. He sent an angel to try to stop him. Balaam and his two servants couldn't see the angel, but the donkey that Balaam was riding saw him. As they traveled along, suddenly the angel was standing in the donkey's way with a sword in his hand. When the donkey saw the angel, he turned from the path and ran into a field. Balaam was angry with the donkey and hit him and made him go the way he directed.

A little while later, the angel was again standing in the donkey's way. This time it was in a vineyard where grapes were grown and there was a wall on both sides of the path. When the donkey saw the angel, he ran into one of the walls and hurt Balaam's foot. Again Balaam became angry and hit the animal. Balaam still hadn't seen the angel.

A little further on, the angel stood in the way again. This time there was no way to turn, so the donkey fell down under Balaam. Balaam was so angry that he hit the donkey with a stick.

Now something very strange happened. The Lord opened the donkey's mouth and he talked to his master. "What have I done to you that made you hit me these three times?" he asked.

Balaam may have been surprised, the Bible doesn't say, but he answered, "Because you've not obeyed me. Why, if I had a sword here in my hand instead of a stick I would have killed you!"

"Have I ever disobeyed you before?" the donkey asked.

"No," Balaam admitted.

Then the Lord let Balaam see the angel with the sword in his hand, just as the donkey had been seeing him all along. Balaam bowed his head and fell down flat on the ground.

"Why have you hit your donkey these three times?" the angel asked. "I have stood in his way because you did not do as God commanded. The donkey saw me and turned from me three times. If she had not done this, I would surely have killed you."

"I have done wrong," Balaam said. "I didn't know you were there. If you want me to, I will return home."

"No, go on with the men," the angel said, "but say only what God tells you to say."

So Balaam went on with the princes of Balak.

When King Balak heard that Balaam was on his way, he went out to meet him. "Why didn't you come when I sent for you the first time?" he commanded.

"I'm here now," Balaam answered. "That which the Lord tells me to say will I say."

The next day Balak took Balaam up on a high hill. "See? There are the Israelites," he said.

"Build seven altars here," Balaam said, "and prepare seven oxen and seven rams for sacrifices."

King Balak did as Balaam told him.

"Now, stand by the burnt sacrifice," Balaam said, "and I will go see if the Lord will talk to me."

Balaam climbed up higher on the mountain and went over to where he would be alone, and God came to him there.

"I have prepared seven altars and on each altar have sacrificed a ram and a bullock," Balaam said.

"Return to Balak," God said, "and say what I tell you to say."

Balaam returned to King Balak. "You have brought me here to curse the Israelites," he said. "But how can I curse those whom God has blessed?"

"What are you doing?" King Balak shouted. "I brought you here to curse these people and you bless them instead!"

Then Balaam said, "I can only say what God tells me to say. Come with me and we will ask Him again."

King Balak and Balaam went to another place and built seven altars and sacrificed seven bullocks and seven rams again. Still God did not change His blessing.

King Balak and Balaam went to still another place and built seven altars and sacrificed seven bullocks and seven rams, and still God did not change His blessing.

Finally, King Balak gave up. He knew he couldn't change Balaam's mind. He knew he couldn't get him to curse the Israelites. Balaam was glad that even though he had started out to do what God had not wanted him to do, that God had given him a second chance. He was glad that his donkey had seen the angel. He was glad his donkey had known enough to stop when he saw the sword in the angel's hand. For a little while the donkey was smarter than his master, wasn't he? In fact, for a little while the donkey had even been able to talk with him!

PROGRAM 11
LEARNING TO OBEY

Larger Scripture Lesson: Luke 2:41-52

Scripture for Children's Church: Luke 2:41-43

Object Lesson:

Obeying Our Parents

Object: Toy badge, or something representing law

When boys and girls are told to do something by a grown-up, sometimes they don't like to do it. Sometimes they even get angry. They think it isn't fair for someone bigger than they are to make them do something, especially if they don't want to do it.

However, most rules are made for our own good. If we didn't have rules, lots of people would take advantage of us. We might even take advantage of them, too! We must always obey the laws that the government makes. Usually we are better off because of them.

For instance, what if we didn't have any rules or laws for driving? Why, we'd probably all be dead by now! Cars would be speeding and turning corners from any old lane and there would be wrecks all over town.

The Bible tells us that we should obey the laws of the government. It also tells us that children should obey their parents. If you obey your parents when you are young, it won't be so hard to obey the laws of the government when you grow up.

This is a toy badge, but when you see a real one, you should respect it and be glad that our country is ruled by laws.

Application Story:

Careless Billy

One Saturday Billy was outside playing with his friends. He played and played. He played all afternoon. He didn't notice that the sky was beginning to get darker and that the weather was beginning to get cooler. He didn't notice that first he would get hot from running and then he would get cool when he stopped—hot and cool, hot and cool, all afternoon.

By the time Billy went into the house, he noticed that his throat was a little scratchy, but he didn't do anything for his scratchy throat. He was too busy playing.

After a while, Billy went into the kitchen for a glass of water. When he finished his water, he placed his empty glass on the sink. He forgot that his mother had told him to always put his glass where no one else could get it when he had a sore throat.

That night Billy felt pretty bad. His throat was sore, his head ached, and his chest felt like somebody was standing on it.

"We'd better doctor you up," Billy's mother said, "or you'll get sicker yet."

The next morning, Billy got up bright and early. He felt much better than he had the night before.

"Drink plenty of liquids today, Billy," his mother suggested at breakfast. "We want to chase that old cold away. Also, please use your handkerchief when you cough or sneeze."

"Yes, Mother," Billy said.

Billy drank lots and lots of water and lots and lots of fruit juice that day. Although he felt pretty good, he coughed and sneezed a lot. Usually he forgot to use his handkerchief to catch his germs. He just let them fly all over the room. Now Billy couldn't see the germs flying around, because germs are so tiny that people can't see them, but they are there just the same.

All during the weekend Billy coughed and sneezed and drank liquids. On Monday, Billy was still coughing and sneezing, coughing and sneezing. He had no hanky, of course.

"Billy, cough into your handkerchief," his teacher said.

Billy never remembered. When he did think of it, it was too late. He already had sent his cold germs dancing out into the air, looking for somebody else to move into.

Cough, sneeze. Cough, sneeze. All day Billy coughed and sneezed. He felt pretty good, so he didn't see any reason to stay away from other people. He went right on coughing and sneezing. He never remembered to use his hanky.

Billy played with his friends at school. He played with his friends who lived close to his home. He even played with his two little sisters when he couldn't find anyone else to play with.

On Tuesday, Billy didn't cough and sneeze so much. In fact, his cold was just about gone. You see, Billy was a strong boy. That morning he noticed that Betty and Barbara, his two little sisters, weren't downstairs to eat breakfast when he went down to eat. "Where are Betty and Barbara?" he asked his mother.

"They weren't feeling well this morning, so they're sleeping late. I'm afraid they've caught your cold, Billy."

"Oh, that's too bad," Billy said.

When Billy reached school, he noticed that there weren't many children playing on the playground. When the bell rang and the students went to their classes, he noticed that at least ten of his friends were absent. "That's strange," Billy thought. "I wonder where they all are."

Miss Hagedorn, the teacher, announced that it seemed as though there were a lot of boys and girls out of school today because they were sick with colds.

"Boy!" Billy thought. "First Betty and Barbara and now Don and Skinny, and all the others. It looks like an epi . . . epi . . . demic or something (Billy had heard his dad use that word when he had read an article in the newspaper when a lot of people were sick with typhoid fever) .

Miss Hagedorn cleared her throat. She reached for her handkerchief and sneezed. "Excuse me," she said. "It seems that I am catching a cold, too."

That night after school, Billy opened the front door and called, "I'm home!" But no one came to greet him the way they usually did. "Where is everyone," he wondered.

"We're upstairs, Billy," his mother called.

Billy ran up the steps two at a time. He looked in Betty and Barbara's room. They were both in bed. He went on down the hall to his mother and father's bedroom and looked in there. His mother was lying on her bed, with a box of Kleenex beside her.

"Hello, Billy," she said. "Did you have a good day at school?"

"Yeah," Billy said. "But there sure were a lot of kids absent. Miss Hagedorn said they all had colds."

"That's too bad," his mother said.

"Yeah," Billy answered as he turned to leave the room. "I'm going down to make a sandwich. Okay?"

"Yes, of course. I was going to bake some cookies today, but I didn't feel like it."

"That's too bad, too," Billy said.

As he walked down the steps, he thought, "Funny thing. First, I got a cold and then Betty and Barb and Mom and my friends.

Hum-mm. I wonder . . ." Billy started to sneeze . . . "I wonder if
. . . Ah-ah-ah," . . . he pulled his hanky from his pocket, . . .
"CHEW!"
Bible Story:

Jesus As A Boy

Jesus grew up in the town of Nazareth. His father was a car-
penter who built things out of wood, and he taught Jesus how to
build things, too. Jesus liked to play with the other boys, too,
just as you like to play with your friends. He probably played
different games than you, but he enjoyed them just as much as
you do.

Every year His mother and father traveled to Jerusalem with
their friends and relatives to attend a very special holiday feast,
but Jesus was too young to go.

However, the year that Jesus became 12 years old, His mother
said, "Jesus, now that you are 12, you may go to Jerusalem with
us."

Jesus was happy and excited. He had always wanted to go to
see the beautiful city of Jerusalem and the temple where people
worshiped God. He had heard much about how beautiful it all
was.

Jesus enjoyed His trip to Jerusalem. He explored the city and
He played with the other boys, but the thing He liked most of all
was the beautiful temple. He loved to hear the wise men in the
temple talk about God.

The time passed all too quickly and soon it was time to return
home. All of the people from Nazareth gathered together and
started back. The children walked together and played along the
way. The grownups traveled together, too, discussing all of the
things they had seen and done in Jerusalem. The men usually
were in one part of the group and the women were in another.

After they had traveled most of the day, Mary and Joseph
began to look for Jesus.

"Where is Jesus?" Mary asked Joseph.

"I don't know. I haven't seen Him all day," Joseph answered.
"I thought you knew where He was."

"Have you seen Jesus?" they asked His friends.

"No, we haven't seen Him," His friends answered.

"Have you seen Jesus?" they asked all of the grownups.

"No, we haven't seen Him," all the grownups answered.

Mary became frightened. "Where can He be? We've asked everyone and no one has seen Him all day."

"If He's not with us, we must have left Him back in Jerusalem,"," Joseph said. "We'd better go back and look for Him."

"Don't worry. He's a big boy now," one of Mary's friends said. "You'll find Him."

Mary and Joseph turned around and went back to Jerusalem. When they got there, they hunted everywhere. They went back to where they had stayed. "No. We haven't seen Jesus," the people said. They went to the market place. "No. We haven't seen a 12-year-old boy who is lost," the people there said. They hunted for Jesus for three days.

After they had searched every place they could think of, Joseph said, "I know where we haven't looked! We haven't looked in the temple!"

Mary and Joseph ran to the temple as fast as they could. They looked at every boy they saw there, but they didn't see Jesus. Finally someone said, "Oh, yes, I know who you must mean. There is a boy talking to the teachers over there. Perhaps He is the boy you are looking for."

Mary and Joseph walked over to the group of men who were listening to a young boy who was standing among them. Sure enough, it was Jesus. Mary and Joseph hurried over to Him.

"Where have you been?" Mary asked. "Why have you done this to us? We have been afraid that we had lost you and have been looking all over for you."

"Why have you been hunting for me?" Jesus asked. "Didn't you know that I would be about my Father's business?"

"We must go home now," Joseph said.

Jesus got up and looked at all the wise men with whom He had been talking. "Thank you for talking with Me," He said. "I'll be back next year."

"Good-bye. We will be glad to see you," they answered.

Jesus and Mary and Joseph went back to their home in Nazareth where Jesus lived until He was 30 years old. Even though He knew that He was the Son of God and that there was something very special that He would have to do, He obeyed His mother, Mary, and His earthly father, Joseph. He was a good son who grew up tall and straight and learned many things and made many friends.

PROGRAM 12
BEING OBEDIENT

Larger Scripture Lesson: Genesis 22:1-14

Scripture for Children's Church: Genesis 22:7-9

Object Lesson:

Disobedience Has To Be Punished

Object: A switch

Sometimes boys and girls are naughty. Sometimes you disobey your parents and do things you shouldn't do. When you do this, your parents are unhappy and they have to punish you. They punish you so you'll learn what they want you to do. It is a part of training.

There are many ways boys and girls can be punished when they are disobedient. One way is to be sent to your room. One way is not to get any dessert. One way is to have to sit in a corner. One way is to be spanked.

This switch could be used to punish somebody. It is long and green and will reach a long way and not break when it is bent.

I hope no one ever has to use a switch on you!

Application Story:

Spot's Trick

Spot is a very special dog. That is, he is very special to Paul. Paul loves Spot more than almost anything in the whole wide world.

He doesn't care if Spot is a mongrel. He doesn't care that Spot is such a mixture of different breeds of dogs that even the veterinarian has trouble deciding what kind of dog he is!

Spot is neither too big nor too little. He is just right for Paul. His legs are rather short, but he can run as fast as Paul can run.

Spot is mostly white except for some brown spots dotted here and there. One of these spots encircles his left eye, making him look like he is winking at you. His tail is long and curls into a round letter "o". It wags most of the time; and when Spot's tail wags, his whole body wags, too!

One day, not long ago, Paul decided that Spot should learn some tricks.

"Let's learn how to come when I call you, first," Paul said. "Come!"

Spot cocked his head to one side. Then he realized that Paul had a dog biscuit in his hand, and he trotted over to gobble it up.

They practiced the trick many times.

When the biscuits were all gone, Paul ran into the house to get some more. He was gone only a few minutes, but when he returned to the yard he couldn't find Spot anywhere.

He looked to his right. He looked to his left.

Oh, no! There was Spot right in the middle of the street, staring up at a cat that he had evidently chased up a tree.

"Spot! Spot!" Paul yelled. "You'll get run over!"

Paul heard the motor of an approaching car. It was coming toward Spot. Paul could tell that the driver didn't see the dog.

"Come, Spot! Come!" Paul yelled.

Spot cocked his head. Paul was giving him his command. Up he jumped to obey. And just in the nick of time. The car zoomed on, but Spot was safe in Paul's arms.

Paul was glad that he had taught Spot the trick. But mostly he was glad because Spot was obedient and had obeyed him.

Bible Story:

Abraham, A Man Who Obeyed God

One day, long ago, God spoke to Abram.

"Abram," He said, "I want you to go away from your home here in Haran. I will show you where I want you to go. I will bless you. In fact, I will bless the whole world through you!"

Abram trusted God. He called to his wife, "Come, Sarai," he said. "God has told me that He wants us to leave Haran. Let's pack all of our things. We will take my nephew Lot and all of our servants and animals and head south into the land of Canaan."

Abram and Sarai packed all their things and started on their trip. They were nomads. This means that they lived in tents and they traveled all of the time. When they decided that they wanted to stay in one place for a while, they did. When they decided that they wanted to move on, they moved on.

Every time Abram and his family stopped for awhile, Abram built an altar to God and sacrificed animals to Him. God spoke to Abram several times.

Once God told Abram, "I am giving you all of this land. It is for you and your children and your children's children and all of their children."

Abram knew that God owned all of this land. In fact, He had created it. But Abram wondered what God meant by his children and his grandchildren and his great grandchildren. Abram was 75 years old, and he didn't have any children!

A long time passed. God talked with Abram many times. One of these times He told Abram that his name should no longer be Abram. "From now on it will be 'Abraham'," God said. (Abram means High Father; Abraham means Father of a Multitude.)

God also told Abraham, "Sarai's name will be changed to 'Sarah'." (Sari means Princely; Sarah means Princess.)

"Walk before Me and be perfect," God said. "And I will make you the father of many nations and many kings. The land of Canaan will be for your people forever."

Twenty-five years after God had first talked to Abraham and promised him a son, God kept that promise.

Abraham and Sarah had a baby boy.

They named him "Isaac" which means "Laughter." This was a good name for their baby because they were both so happy to have him.

Isaac grew up to be a handsome young man. Abraham loved him very much. Now God was going to test his faith in Him.

One day He called, "Abraham, take your only and beloved son Isaac and go into the land of Moriah. When you are there, I will tell you which mountain I want you to go to. I want you to offer Isaac as a burnt offering to me."

Abraham groaned. He didn't want to obey God. He loved God, but he loved his son Isaac, too. Still Abraham obeyed God.

Early the next morning, Abraham, Isaac, and two young servants left their tents. They carried cut wood and fire for the sacrifice.

After they had traveled three days, Abraham gazed up at a mountain. God instructed him to make his sacrifice there.

"You stay here," Abraham told his servants. "Isaac and I will go up and worship alone."

Abraham and Isaac climbed the mountain together. Abraham carried the fire and knife; Isaac carried the wood.

"Father, we have the fire and the knife and the wood, but where is the lamb for the burnt offering?" Isaac asked his father.

"My son, God will provide Himself a lamb," Abraham answered.

They reached the top of the mountain. They built an altar. They put the wood on the altar.

Isaac realized at last that he himself was going to be the sacrifice. Abraham tied him up with a rope. He placed him on the altar. Isaac lay very still. He was an obedient son. Abraham clutched the knife in his hand. Up, up, up went his arm. High above his head he held the blade that was going to take the life of his son. He steeled himself, ready to plunge the knife into Isaac's heart.

"Abraham! Abraham! Stop! Don't kill Isaac. You have proven to me that you really do love me because you have obeyed me in the hardest possible thing for you to do."

Tears rolled down Abraham's cheeks. He was so happy that God had called him and he didn't have to kill his son.

Then, all of a sudden, he heard a ram. "Baa—a—a." It was caught in the bushes nearby. This was the sacrifice that God had provided.

God said, "Because you have done this, Abraham, I will surely bless you."

This story happened almost four thousand years ago. Now we can see through history how God has kept His promise to Abraham. Remember that God said that the whole world would be blessed through Abraham? A little over nineteen hundred years ago a baby boy by the name of Jesus was born to Mary, a young Hebrew woman, a descendant of Abraham.

Jesus was also the Son of God. He grew up and preached to the people and taught them. He told them that it was God's will and purpose to give eternal life to everyone who would trust in Him. Some of the people wouldn't listen to Jesus, and one day they seized Him and nailed Him to a cross to die.

Jesus didn't have to let them do this to Him, but He knew that this was the only way that people could be saved from their sins. Because He was the Son of God, He alone was able to overcome sin and death.

He did this for you and for me and for everyone who will accept Him and trust in Him as Savior.

This is what God meant when He told Abraham that the whole world would be blessed through Him. God knew that Abraham loved Him and He knew that Abraham would obey Him. Aren't you glad he did?

PROGRAM 13
SHARING WITH OTHERS

Larger Scripture Lesson: Luke 15:11-32

Scripture for Children's Church: Luke 15:11-13

Object Lesson:

Unselfish People Are Happy People

Object: Enough cookies for everybody

I have some cookies. I didn't have to tell you about my cookies. I could have hidden them so no one would know that I have them. I could sneak in where I'd hidden them every once in a while and get one for myself and eat it. The trouble is, I wouldn't enjoy these cookies nearly as much if I had to eat them that way.

It would be much nicer for me, and you, too, if I shared my cookies. Then you would be happy, and I'd be happy because you were!

Sometimes people don't like to share. If they don't, they are selfish. Selfish people are never as happy as people who share! God wants us to be unselfish. He wants us to share.

Application Story:

We Believe In Sharing

It was not fast moving, but gently rippling as it meandered slowly through the valley. The water's surface was smooth and shiny. Shadows of the large pin oak trees and berry bushes hung dark green in the quiet softness of Elk River.

Corky lazily cast out his fishing line. It landed with a plunk. Patiently he waited for a nibble. Then, without any warning, he felt a jerk and a steady pull. "I've got a bite!," he thought. He reeled in the line, carefully maneuvering his pole so he wouldn't lose his prize. The tug on the line thrilled the freckle faced boy as he managed to draw the fighting fish up close to the bank.

He drew in a deep breath when he got a closer look. Oh, boy! He had never seen such a whopper. Wait until Dad and Mom and Ted see this! It must weigh five pounds!

Slowly, slowly, Corky managed to pull the fish in close. Deftly he placed his net under the fish to claim it for his own.

It flopped helplessly as Corky triumphantly strung him on the heavy cord and tied him up. "I'll save him to surprise Dad and Ted," he thought as he secured the cord with the big fish on it to a stone beside the river. Corky's big brown eyes shined happily as he looked into the water and admired his catch.

He looked upstream and downstream. He didn't see his dad or his younger brother, Ted. "I'll save mine and show it last. Won't they be surprised?" he thought.

Soon Corky was basking in the sunshine enjoying the twitter of the black birds and the cooling current of fresh air. He loved to fish. It was fun to come to Green Mountain Valley with his family. It was fun to be able to land a fish like the one he had caught that morning. It was fun to eat them, too, when they all gathered around the old table on the screened-in porch of their cabin.

Working his way up the river, Corky cast his line out and reeled it back. Suddenly he felt the jerk which he had been hoping for. Again he pulled in a fine catch. "This must be my lucky day," Corky thought as he headed back down the bank to add this fish to his first one." I hope Dad and Ted are doing as well. Well, almost, anyway."

Two more times Corky felt the familiar tug and pulled in a fish. Two more times he strung his prize with the others. His bright brown eyes revealed his pride.

"According to my stomach, it must be time for lunch," he thought and he started back toward the little vacation cabin where his family was staying. The pungent smell of frying fish met him as he went inside. He washed his hands and face.

"Hi, Mom. Can I help?" he asked.

Soon Dad and Ted joined them and washed up. They all sat down and Dad asked the blessing.

"Thank You for this fine vacation, Lord," he prayed. "Please bless this food and make it nourishing for our bodies. And help us to share all the blessings that we have. Amen."

Hungrily everyone finished off the meal.

"Catch anything?" Dad asked Corky.

"Boy! Wait until you see!" Corky bragged.

Soon the dishes were cleared away and the boys and their

father were back out on the bank, busy once more with their rods and reels.

It wasn't long until they had separated again. Dad was working his way downstream, and Ted was staying close to the cabin. Corky was working his way downstream.

He soon found a comfortable spot where he could sit. He enjoyed watching the little fish chase his lure, but he really got excited when he saw a big fish swim up to investigate it. The afternoon didn't prove to be as profitable as the morning was, though. Consoling himself that at least he had four good-sized catches, he went to get them. Cleaning them wasn't much fun, but the boys had learned from the very beginning that what they caught, they cleaned. Corky wanted everyone to see his fish before he cleaned them.

Hearing footsteps behind him, he turned to see a barefoot, overalled boy about his own age. "Hi!" the boy greeted him.

"Hi! I'm Corky. What's your name?" Corky asked.

"They call me Limey," the boy answered. "I live up there in the hills," pointing to the east.

"Yeah, I think I know the place," Corky said. "But the last time I was up there it was empty."

"We just moved in," Limey said. "We couldn't pay any rent at the last place. And we don't have to pay any rent up here. Mom said the cabin was good enough until it gets too cold. Where do you live?"

"Well, actually, we live in town," Corky answered. "We're out here on our vacation. It's really a great place, isn't it?"

"Yeah, I guess so," Limey said. "That is, if you don't *have* to live out here!"

"Funny how we are, isn't it?" mused Corky. "Anything we have to do we hardly ever like, do we?"

"Do you have any brothers or sisters?" Limey asked.

"One brother younger than me. His name's Ted. Do you?"

"Yeah. I have three brothers and three sisters. And I'm the oldest. They're all too little to help much, but I come down here to the river and catch what fish I can. We get sort of tired of it, but it's sure better'n nothing!"

"How many did you catch today?" Corky asked.

"Today's been a bad day. I only have this little measley one here. It's almost too small to keep, but I guess I'd better."

Corky began to do some thinking. As he thought, they headed toward the fish house.

"Come on over to the fish house and let's clean our fish," he said.

"I usually clean mine in the river," Limey said. "I don't come over here often. But, thanks."

The two boys went up to the little screened-in building and closed the door behind them.

"Smells pretty awful, doesn't it?" Corky asked.

"Yeah," Limey answered, "but you get used to it. Say! You really caught some big ones, didn't you?"

"Yeah," answered Corky, trying not to act too proud and pleased with himself.

After the fish were cleaned, Corky turned to Limey.

"Say, Limey. I've been thinking. This'll be just about enough for you and your family tonight. Why don't you take my fish home with you?"

"You really mean it? I don't want to take your fish. After all, you caught them."

"Oh, we'll have plenty, anyway," Corky said. "Ted and Dad have been out today, too. Besides, Mom has some bacon or something in case we don't have enough."

"Boy, thanks," Limey said. "Wait until Ma and the kids see this. They'll sure be tickled. You're sure you mean it?"

"Sure, I'm sure," Corky chuckled as he washed the fish and wrapped them in wax paper.

"Thanks, Corky. You're a swell guy!" Limey said as he accepted the package. "I hope you stay around a while. Maybe we could fish together."

"We'll be here the rest of the week," Corky called, watching Limey turn and hurry toward home. "Come on over any time."

The screen door slammed behind Limey just as he passed Ted.

"Hey, Corky, look what I caught!" Ted exclaimed as he came running up with a fish flopping in his net. "Where's yours?"

Corky looked at Ted's fish. It wasn't nearly as big as two of his own had been. "But why ruin Ted's enjoyment," he thought. "Oh, they all got away," he answered.

"Where are those fish you were bragging about at lunch, Corky?" Dad asked, joining his sons.

"Well, Dad, like I told Ted. I guess I let them get away."

Dad grinned because he remembered the boy he had seen when he came up to the fish house. Pretty handsome package of fish the boy was carrying! He looked mighty happy as he hurried away.

Then Dad said, "Well, Ted and I have plenty for all of us, don't we, Ted? We believe in sharing, don't we, Son?" Then he winked at Corky and put a big strong arm around him.

Corky looked up at his had. Did he guess what had happened to the fish? They grinned at each other. Dad was a pretty smart fellow.

"We sure do, Dad!"

Bible Story:

The Lost Son

One of the many stories Jesus told while He was here on earth was to show the people how happy God and even all of his angels are when one person is sorry for his sins and accepts Jesus as his Savior. The name of the story is "The Lost Son."

Once there was a very rich man. This man lived in a large, beautiful house. He owned much land and many animals. He even had servants to take care of his house, his land and his animals. The man also had two sons.

One day the youngest son decided that he wanted to leave home. There wasn't anything interesting to do and he was bored. He said to his father, "When you die, you'll leave me some money. Why can't I have that money now? I want to leave home and go out into the world."

The father was sad. He didn't want his son to leave home. He loved both of his boys very much. Even though he would still have his older son with him, he knew that he would be lonely for his younger son.

However, the father was kind. He wanted to let his son do what he wanted to do. He divided up his property and possessions and gave a lot of money to the boy.

Soon the young man was all packed. He went away to a country a long way from home. There he met many friends— or people he thought were friends. They really liked him because they learned how much money he had.

The young man and his "friends" spent money on rich food and drink. They wasted it.

"It's mine," the young man said to himself. "And I have a right to spend it like I want."

Since he didn't work to earn any money, and since he spent what he had on a lot of foolishness, he soon had no money left at all. Now the people who had helped him spend it all disappeared. He learned that they didn't like him for himself at all. It was only his money that they had liked.

Now he had no money, no home, no food, and no friends.

On top of all that, a great famine was in the land. The crops had not grown, and everybody was short of money and food. He couldn't find a job because there weren't any. He didn't know what to do. After a long time, he finally got a job feeding pigs. This was just about the lowest kind of job there was. He got so hungry he almost ate some of the pigs' food!

"How low I have fallen!" he said one day. "Why, at my father's house even the hired servants have more than enough to eat. I have an idea. I'll go back home. I'll tell my father how sorry I am for having been such a bad son. I'll tell him I am no longer good enough to be called his son any more. I'll tell him I have sinned before him and before heaven. 'Make me one of your hired servants,' I'll say."

The young man got up quickly and headed back toward home. "I wonder how father will receive me," he thought. "I hope he'll be glad to see me. He is a good man. I know he will treat me well."

He was not disappointed. He didn't know it, but his father had been looking for him all of the time he had been gone. He had been hoping all of the time that his son would return.

On the road, when the young man was still quite a way from his old home, he saw a man looking up the road toward him. Suddenly he saw the man waving his arms happily. It was his father.

The older man ran to meet his son. He put his arms around his son's neck and hugged and kissed him. Tears of happiness rolled down his cheeks.

"Oh, father," the young man said. "I am no longer worthy to be called your son. I have spent all of my money foolishly, and I am hungry and have no place to stay. . . ."

The father didn't let him finish his sentence. He called out to his servants. "Go get the prize calf and kill it. We're going to have a feast! We are going to celebrate the return of my son. I thought he was dead, but he is alive and has returned home! Put a ring on his finger and shoes on his feet!"

So the feasting began.

In the meantime, the older son was out working in the field. "What's going on?" he asked a servant. "Why is everybody singing and dancing?"

"Why, your brother has returned and your father is giving a party because he is glad he is alive and safe."

Do you know how the older brother reacted? He got angry and refused to go into the house. His father came out to see what was the matter.

"Please come in," the father begged.

"Look," the younger man answered, "I have worked like a slave for you and have not once disobeyed you, but what have you given me? You haven't given me even a goat so I could have a feast for my friends! Your younger son has gone out and squandered away all of your money and when he comes home, he gets a prize calf killed for him!"

"My son," the father said, "you are always home and everything I have is yours. But we had the feast for your brother because he was dead and now he is alive; he was lost, but now he is found."

That is the end of Jesus' story. He wants us to learn some lessons from it. He wants us to be like the father, who was kind and forgiving. He doesn't want us to be like the older brother, who didn't want to share. We always want to make Jesus happy by being kind and by sharing.

PROGRAM 14
FORGIVING OTHERS

Larger Scripture Lesson: Matthew 18:21-35
Scripture for Children's Church: Matthew 18:32, 33
Object Lesson:

God Wants Us To Forgive Others

Object: Lighted Candle

God wants us to forgive others. He doesn't want us to hold anything against anybody. You can say you forgive somebody, but it doesn't count if it doesn't come from your heart. You really have to mean it. God knows our hearts. He knows if we really mean it or not.

If we forgive somebody, it means that we will forget all about it. It will be just like it had never happened at all.

It will be just like the flame on this candle. Now it is there. (Blow out flame on candle.) Now it isn't. And that particular flame is gone forever. There will be other flames, but this one will never exist again.

If you are sincere when you forgive someone, you will completely forgive the person for what he has done. It will be like he never did it at all.

This is the way God forgives. When we ask Him to forgive our sins, He has promised He will forgive them. "If we confess our sins, he is faithful and just to forgive us our sins, and to cleanse us from all unrighteousness" I John 1:9.

Application Story:

Surprise Party

Jeannie and Gladys were beginning to get restless. The party time had been set for 7:30, and now it was 8 o'clock. Not once had they heard the sound of girlish voices on the front porch.

Not once had the door bell rung to announce the arrival of a guest. They were very disappointed.

"Let's wait 15 more minutes, and if no one comes by then—well, phooey. We'll just forget it," Gladys said.

It was Jeannie's birthday and Gladys had worked hard all day to make it special. She had baked a chocolate cake with pink icing and had written "Happy Birthday, Jeannie" across the top. It was a beautiful cake and Gladys had been very proud of it. She had made pink lemonade, too. She had thought it would be a grand party.

She had cleaned the house and set out plates and cups and napkins. She had prepared a flower centerpiece for the table with pink and white streamers reaching from it to the outer edges of the table.

She stepped back from her handiwork to see if everything was in order. "Yes, it looked perfect," Gladys thought.

Jeannie had gone to visit an aunt for the day and Gladys was glad because there was no possibility of her dropping in and finding out about the surprise.

Gladys had called all the girls in their Sunday School class and arrangements had been made for them to arrive at 7:30. Jeannie was supposed to come over at 7:45. If everything had worked out like it was supposed to, Jeannie would have found everybody waiting to call out "Surprise!" when she came in. As it turned out, only Gladys was waiting—and she was too unhappy to even smile when Jeannie arrived.

The surprise had been ruined. Gladys felt like crying. She had gone to so much trouble and work to have a nice party for her friend. And now it was all ruined.

"No, it's not," Jeannie insisted. "I still had my surprise and I think you're swell to do all of this for me. Maybe something has happened to keep the others from coming."

"They could have called," Gladys pouted. "I don't think it's very nice of them."

Gladys was getting more upset. She felt herself getting madder and madder. Finally, at 8:15, she gave up. It was obvious that no one was coming. She stood up and started putting the napkins and dishes away.

"I have an idea," Jeannie offered. "We can still have a party and then all your work won't be lost. Let's go over to Mrs. Jackman's and take the cake. It's too bad your folks aren't home. They could go with us. Mrs. Jackman never gets out and she always likes to have company."

"Well, okay," Gladys said. "After all, it's your cake. You should be able to do what you want to with it."

"We'd better call first and see if she's still up," Jeannie suggested.

"Why bother?" Gladys pouted. "Her lights are on. I can see them from the dining room window."

Mrs. Jackman was an invalid who lived next door to Gladys. Although she wasn't able to walk and had to sit in a wheelchair all day, she was always pleasant and cheerful. The girls stopped in to see her quite often, and she was always pleased to see them. They were always sure of a welcome.

Gladys picked up some napkins and the pitcher full of punch. Jeannie carried her birthday cake, complete with candles. They walked across to Mrs. Jackman's front door and Jeannie pressed the buzzer.

"Coming!" they heard from inside the house. "Who's there, please?"

"It's Gladys and Jeannie," Gladys called back. Then they heard the click of the night latch being unlocked. The front door swung open.

"Well, this is a pleasant surprise," Mrs. Jackman said when she saw the girls with the cake and punch. "Are we going to have a party?"

"Yeah," Gladys said. "Nobody came to ours."

Jeannie hurriedly explained, "You see, Mrs. Jackman, today is my birthday. Gladys worked hard all day to get ready for a party she was having for me. She baked this cake 'n everything. And then nobody came! We thought we'd just have our party anyway and came over to share it with you!"

"Well, how thoughtful of you," Mrs. Jackman exclaimed as she wheeled herself back out of the girls' way. "I'd be delighted to join your party. And I wonder, too, would you like to ask Mr. Grant? He's all alone in his apartment upstairs."

"Sure. We have lots of cake and punch," Gladys said as she headed toward the steps to go up and invite Mr. Grant. Soon the two of them were back downstairs. Mr. Grant's face was bright and eager.

"My! My!" he said, "this is so nice. I was just beginning to feel sorry for myself because I thought everybody had forgotten me!" He gingerly sat at the place Jeannie pointed out for him and Gladys pushed Mrs. Jackman up to the table beside him. The girls sat down opposite them.

"Would you like to ask the blessing, Mrs. Jackman?" Gladys asked.

They all bowed their heads and closed their eyes.

Mrs. Jackman prayed. "Dear God," she said. "We thank Thee for these two thoughtful girls and for this fine birthday cake. Please bless us as we have this party together. Mr. Grant and I want to thank You for seeing to it that we got to come, too! In Jesus' Name. Amen."

When they lifted their heads and opened their eyes, Jeannie and Gladys looked at each other. Gladys could see that Jeannie wasn't disappointed because the other girls hadn't come. Gladys almost felt happy, too. After all, if the others had come, Mrs. Jackman and Mr. Grant couldn't have. And, anyway, they probably all had good reasons for not coming.

All of a sudden she wasn't resentful anymore. Everything had turned out better than she had expected! She was almost glad the other girls hadn't shown up.

"Make a wish, Jeannie, and blow out the candles!" she said. "We want some cake!"

Bible Story:

The Unforgiving Servant

Jesus was teaching His disciples. He told them many things. One of the things He talked about was forgiving other people.

"How often should I forgive someone?" Peter asked Him. "Is seven times enough?" Seven times seemed like a lot to Peter.

"No," Jesus answered, "seven times is not enough. You should forgive 70 times seven times!"

Then Jesus told Peter and the other disciples a story about a man who was unforgiving.

"There was once a king," Jesus said, "who decided he would check on how much his servants owed him. He discovered that there was one servant who owed him almost ten million dollars.

"'Bring this servant to me,' the king commanded.

"When the man was brought to him, the king said, 'I want you to repay me all of the money you have borrowed from me.'

'Oh, Master,' the servant said, 'I can't. I don't have the money to pay you back.'

"The king said to his other servants: 'Take this man. Take his wife and his children. Take all of his possessions. Sell him and his family and give me the money. This way I will be repaid.'

"The man fell down on his knees before the king."

" 'Please spare me,' he begged. 'Have patience and I will pay you all I owe!'

"The king felt sorry for the servant. 'Get up,' he said, 'and don't worry. Your debt is forgiven. You won't have to pay it, and I won't take you or your family to be sold.'

"The servant left the king.

"Right after that, he went to a man who owed him some money. It wasn't nearly as much as what he had owed the king.

" 'Pay me what you owe me!' he commanded.

"His fellow servant fell down at his feet. 'Have patience with me and I'll pay you everything,' he begged.

"But the man had no patience.

" 'Take him to prison,' he shouted, 'until he pays me.'

"When the man's fellow servants saw what he had done, they told the king.

"The king called him again.

" 'You are wicked," the king said. 'I forgave you all you owed me because I felt sorry for you. Why didn't you feel sorry for someone who owed you something? I had pity on you. Why didn't you have pity on him?'

"The king was very angry.

" 'Take this man to jail!' he commanded. 'And make him stay there until he can pay me!' "

Jesus explained the story to his disciples and told them, "God wants you to be forgiving like the king and not unforgiving like the servant."

Jesus knows what it is to be forgiving. When He was hanging on the cross being crucified, he didn't hold it against the people who were killing Him. Even when He was in great pain, He called out, "Father, forgive them, for they don't understand what they are doing."

Jesus is our example. He wants us to be like Him. We need to learn to be forgiving, too. He understands us and can help us. When we feel hate or dislike in our hearts, we should pray and ask God to forgive us because it is wrong to hate someone. Then we should ask Him to help us to forgive that person.

If Jesus is our example, we must learn to be like Him.

PROGRAM 15
REVERENCE IN CHURCH

Larger Scripture Lesson: 2 Samuel 7, 1 Kings 6, 1 Chronicles 28

Scripture for Children's Church: 2 Samuel 7:1-3

Object Lesson:

God's House

Object: A toy church or a picture of a church

God is everywhere. He is in your heart if you have accepted Jesus as your Savior. He doesn't need a house like this for Himself. He needs one for YOU!

Our church is God's house. It is a special place where you can come to talk about God and learn about Him. It is a place where you can sing songs to Him and about Him. It is a place where you can be with other people who love God, too.

When we come to church to worship God and learn more about Him, sometimes we are bothered by people who are what we call "irreverent." This means that they do not treat something of God with respect. When people run in the church or talk loudly, they are showing that they don't have much respect for God.

Some boys and girls do not have a church where they can worship God. We should learn to love and respect our church and show God that we appreciate having it.

Application Story:

Janet's Prayer Is Answered

"It seems like I'm always getting into trouble at church," Janet told her friend, Susie. "I can't do anything any more. It's 'don't do this' and 'don't do that' so much I get tired of it."

Janet and Susie were standing outside the church waiting for their folks.

"That old Mrs. Stevens bawls me out every time I do anything," Janet complained. "It's no fun to come to church any more."

"I don't know, Jan," Susie answered. "You'll probably get mad at me for saying this, but you do make an awful lot of noise during our group period in Sunday School. I could hardly hear Mrs. Stevens today. And you know nobody is supposed to run in church—not even little kids. . . ."

Susie didn't get to finish before Janet cut in. "Fine friend you are, siding with the grownups. I thought you were my pal."

"Well, I am, and like our lesson said today, 'A friend loveth at all times. . . .'"

Janet cut in again. "Is that what our lesson was about today? I never can understand what Mrs. Stevens is talking about."

"Well, maybe you could, if you'd listen a little better," Susan said as she left to join her parents who were just coming out of church. "See you tonight, Jan," she called.

"Yeah. See you tonight," Janet answered, sort of under her breath. "She's sure a smart aleck. She thinks she's smart," she muttered.

With a flip of her long brown hair she turned to go back inside to see if she could find her own folks.

"That was a very good sermon today," Mr. Browne, Janet's father, said in the car on their way home. "At least what I could hear of it. Janet, you are too big to be so much trouble during church. If you don't straighten up, I'm going to march you right out one of these days and give you a spanking you won't forget."

"I didn't do anything," Janet defended herself.

"Do you call wiggling and squirming and rattling papers and mouthing messages to your friends nothing?" Dad answered. "You just mind my words, young lady."

Janet felt blue and dejected when she got home. She went into her room to change her clothes, but she heard her folks talking in the kitchen.

"That young lady better change her ways, or I might as well stop going to church," she heard her father say. "Dr. Woods preaches good sermons, but I can't get much out of them with Janet acting like she's out in the park somewhere."

Janet heard her mother answer. "I know. She bothers me, too. And I'm really embarrassed when I know she's disturbing people around us, but she's almost too big to spank. I really don't know what to do about her. We were sitting by the Hydes today. I was just sure Mrs. Hyde was going to make a decision for Christ today. I hope Janet's behavior didn't keep her from doing it."

Janet felt crushed. Tears of dejection ran down her cheeks and bounced off into her pillow. She really had been a bad girl in church.

"I'm going to try to do better," she promised herself as she got up and went into the kitchen.

That night at church Janet really did behave a little better—for a while at least. Then she forgot all about it. She was sitting next to her friend, Agnes, and they sang songs from the hymnal just like the grownups. Then all during the Scripture reading, Janet and Agnes whispered. When the sermon began, they tried to see which of them could balance her pencil on her finger the longest. Of course the pencils clinked to the floor several times. Janet realized how much of a disturbance they were making when she happened to catch her mother's eye.

"I've got to be quiet," she whispered to Agnes.

It was very hard to sit still. It seemed like Dr. Woods preached for ages. Finally, everyone stood to sing the invitation hymn. Even though they sang four stanzas, no one went forward.

That night after Janet was ready for bed, Mrs. Browne came to her room.

"I'd like to talk with you, Janet," she said as she closed the door behind her. "You were very disrespectful and irreverent in church again tonight. You seemed to have formed a very bad habit. Do you realize that when you are disobedient and disrespectful that you are sinning against God? It seems especially bad to me when you do it in His house. . . ."

"You not only disturb your father and me," Mother continued, "but everyone else who is sitting around us. And I'm sure you don't get anything out of church yourself. What do you think your father and I should do about you? We can't change you. Only you can do that. We can punish you and make you act different, but that wouldn't really change you on the inside. Only you can change yourself—only you and God."

Janet felt sad. She thought she had only been having a little fun before, and she had enjoyed all the attention she was getting.

"I'm truly sorry, Mother. Really I am. I'll try to do better next Sunday."

"Thank you, Janet. I knew you'd understand if I explained it to you. But something like this can become a real habit. I suggest that we pray about it and ask God to help you to be quiet and reverent and respectful in His house. God can help you, if you'll let Him."

Janet and her mother knelt beside Janet's bed. Both of them prayed that God would help her to love Him enough to obey Him and be reverent in His house.

All week Janet prayed to God about her behavior at church. "Forgive me, please, God, for being so naughty and help me to love You so much that I will be quiet and respectful in Your house. With Your help, I know I can do much better."

The next Sunday Janet behaved so well in Sunday School that Mrs. Stevens complimented her on her good behavior. Janet liked this kind of attention much more than the kind she had been getting!

During the worship services, she behaved pretty well, but after a while she forgot and started wiggling. Then she remembered what her mother had said about God helping her to change, and she asked God to help her not to be so restless. She settled back and listened to what Dr. Woods was saying.

"Come unto Me, and I will give you rest."

"Why, she hadn't realized that Jesus had said He would help her when she got tired. Do you suppose He meant tired in church?" she thought. "Is that what that verse meant? She'd have to remember it and ask mother later."

Right now she was busy turning to the hymn they were going to sing. She happened to look over at Mrs. Hyde, who was picking up her Bible and purse. Then Janet saw her heading down the aisle and taking the preacher's hand.

Janet prayed silently again. This time she said, "Thank You, God, for helping Mrs. Hyde to go up in front of everybody and tell them that she loves Jesus. And thank You for helping me to sit still better, too!"

Bible Story:

David Wants To Build A House For God

David was king over all Israel. God had blessed him and had taken care of him. David had a beautiful palace to live in and many servants to care for it. He had a family and many friends. David appreciated all of the things God had given him.

One day, he called the prophet, Nathan, to him.

"Nathan," he said, "I live in a house built of beautiful cedar wood, but God has no house. What do you think I should do about it?"

Nathan answered quickly, "Build God a temple if that is what you want to do. God will surely bless you."

That night while Nathan was asleep, God came to him in a dream.

"Nathan," God said, "I have a message for you to take to David. I have not had a house since I dwelt in the tabernacle Moses and the people built for Me when I rescued them from Egypt. But have I asked for a house of cedar? Go to David and tell him that I took him away from herding sheep to become ruler of the people of Israel. Remind him how I have blessed and protected him.

"Tell David that I will bless all his family that lives after him. Tell him I will establish a kingdom for his family. In fact, tell him that his kingdom will reign forever!"

God meant that the heavenly kingdom would be established through David's family. He meant that Jesus would be a descendant of David's. Jesus would establish the heavenly kingdom. He would be the Son of God and save people from sin so they could live forever with God.

The next morning Nathan went to King David. He told him the message God had given to him. David was very pleased and humble.

"Who am I?" he said to God, "that You should make me such a wonderful promise? Thou art great, O God. There is none like Thee. Thank Thee, for being so good to me."

But God did not want David to build a temple for Him. David had been a soldier and a warrior and had killed many people. God wanted a peaceful man to build His temple.

"Your son, Solomon, will build My temple," God said.

Even though David knew that he was not going to build God's house, he wanted to get things ready so Solomon could start work on it as soon as he became king. He started collecting materials that could be used. He collected millions of dollars worth of materials. There was silver and gold and brass and cedar. There were stones and fine cloth and fine jewels. He also had the architects draw up the temple plans. He worked hard. Millions and millions of dollars were spent for all of the material.

Four years after Solomon became the king, he started the work on God's house.

It took seven and one-half years for almost four thousand men to build the beautiful temple on Mount Moriah. The walls were built of stone which the men cut out at the quarry, and they were covered with cedar. The roof was constructed of beams and planks of cedar. The floor was laid with cypress and the doors were made of cypress, too. The whole inside of the building was overlaid with gold. Yes, it was a very beautiful temple. David had wanted God to have a beautiful house, and now He had one.

Today God doesn't have just one house. He has many. Our church is God's house. It may not be as beautiful as the one David planned and Solomon built, but it is where we come to worship God, and I think it is very beautiful. We sing songs of praise to Him here. We pray. We listen as we hear His Word read and explained. God wants each one of us to love His house and to come to it. He wants us to invite others to come to it, too. He wants all the people to use His house for a place of worship.

PROGRAM 16
ACCEPTING OURSELVES

Larger Scripture Lesson: Luke 15:3-10

Scripture for Children's Church: Luke 15:3-7

Object Lesson:

Things Are Not Always What They Seem

Props: Tongs, rag, rubbing alcohol, water, glass, match.

Procedure: Before Children's Church, (1) make mixture in a glass of one part water to two parts rubbing alcohol, (2) dip the cloth in the mixture and wring it so it does not drip.

During Children's Church, hold the cloth with the tongs so you won't be burned and ignite the cloth at the lower end. (After the flame dies down, you will find that the cloth has not burned.)

Sometimes things are not what they seem. Sometimes we get funny ideas about ourselves. We get what is called an "inferiority complex." This means that we don't think much of ourselves.

It's like this cloth. (Ignite cloth and let the flame burn down.) It probably looked to you like it was going to be all burned up, but, as you can see, it wasn't.

You should take a good look at yourself and look for what God sees in you. He thinks you are worth His giving His Son Jesus to die on the cross to save you from your sins.

If God can accept you, you should be able to accept yourself!

Application Story:

"Doctor" Donald

Sometimes people think they are not as good as other people. Donald was like that.

Actually, Donald could do many things and he had many friends. But Donald had the bad habit of not thinking very highly of himself.

For instance, if he got a "C" on a test at school, even though he had worked really hard and many of the other boys and girls got "C's" or lower, he said, "Boy! I sure am dumb. I can't do anything!"

Or, if he raced with some boys and one beat him, "I sure am dumb," he would say, not taking into consideration that somebody had to lose or that he had outraced some of the other boys.

Donald got into such a bad habit of belittling himself that he really believed it.

One day Johnny, his friend down the street, came by to see him. "Hi!" Johnny said. "Have you got any time? I could sure use your help. I have to fix my bike!"

"Sure," Don answered. He was always glad to do what he could to help his friends.

"You're real smart," Johnny said after Donald had finished fixing the bike. "Thanks a lot."

"Oh, anybody could have done it," Don answered.

"Well, I sure couldn't!" laughed Johnny.

Just then Margie, Johnny's little sister, came out to the garage where the boys were working. She was hugging her doll close to her and crying.

"Johnny, look," she sobbed. "Amanda's head got broken!"

"That's nothing. Don't cry, Margie. We can fix that in nothing flat! Let old Dr. Donald see what he can do," Donald said.

Handing Amanda over to Donald, Margie watched while he smeared glue on the doll's head and stuck the broken piece back where it belonged.

"Go get me some string and we'll put a bandage on her," Donald instructed Margie. "She's going to have to be really quiet for a while. She has just had a very serious operation!"

Donald put a clean cloth around Amanda's head. After he tied the bandage on securely with the string Margie brought him, he handed her the doll. "I'd say she should stay in bed at least the rest of the day," Donald said, standing straight and tall, trying to look as much as possible like a real doctor.

"Thank you, Doctor," Margie said, enjoying the game Donald had been playing. "I'll put her to bed right away!"

"Want to go swimming?" Johnnie asked Donald. "Mom said I could go."

"Sure, but I'll have to check with my mother first."

Soon the boys were on their way. They were lucky to live close to the edge of town and to have a neighbor like Mr. Nance who let them swim in his small lake. Their folks had let them take swimming lessons because Mr. Nance didn't let anyone use the lake unless they were good swimmers. They had passed the test with flying colors, but they still had to swim in pairs. Mr. Nance didn't want anyone to get hurt. The boys were very careful when they swam in the lake.

Already dressed in their trunks, they dashed to the bank.

"Beat you to the raft!" Johnnie called to Don.

"Bet you won't!" Don called back.

Both boys dived in and started swimming for the raft in the middle of the lake. When they reached it, they climbed up. Soon they were diving off and swimming around, having lots of fun.

Suddenly a scream pierced the air. Both boys looked to see what had caused it. Donald's eyes turned toward the bank just in time to see a small figure slide down off of the edge into the lake.

Swiftly he swam over to the spot where he had seen the child go under. He surface dived and searched beneath the water. It didn't take too long to grasp a small arm. With a spurt of power, Donald brought himself and the child up to the surface of the water. Quickly he swam to the shore, pulling the little girl behind him. It was Margie, Johnny's little sister.

"She must've followed us here," Johnny moaned as he helped Donald pull her up onto the land.

"Let me turn her over and get the water out of her lungs," Donald gasped, breathing hard. "You run and tell Mr. Nance and get some help."

Johnny raced toward the farmhouse and Donald worked with Margie, who lay quiet and still on the green grass. Donald remembered what he had learned in life saving. After he checked to see if Margie's tongue was in the right place, he began to give her mouth-to-mouth resuscitation. He put his mouth on hers and blew. He paused. He blew again. Rythmetically he blew and paused until Mr. and Mrs. Nance and Johnny came running up.

"How is she?" Mrs. Nance asked.

Donald didn't answer. He couldn't do what he was doing and talk, too. Soon an ambulance arrived. Donald was glad to hear the siren as it sped down the road toward them. Margie's eyelids fluttered a little.

The doctor in the ambulance ran to the group by the lake. He stooped over to check Margie's pulse. He pressed his stethoscope to listen to her heartbeat. Margie began to move her arms and legs.

"I think she'll be all right now, thanks to you, young man," the doctor said, nodding at Donald. "But we'd better take her to the hospital to watch her for a little while. Would you care to come along?"

Donald and Johnny climbed into the back of the ambulance to be with Margie, who was lying with her eyes wide open now. She whispered something neither of them could hear. Donald put his ear close to her lips.

"You really are a doctor, aren't you, Donald?" the little girl said.

"Well, not exactly," he answered. "But do you know what? I may be some day! I guess I'm not as dumb as I thought I was!"

Bible Story:

The Lost Sheep And The Lost Coin

Jesus often preached and taught while he was out in the countryside and when he was on the city streets. Large crowds would gather and He would tell the people about God and how He had sent Him to save them from their sins. All kinds of people gathered around Him. There were good people and there were bad people. There were people who loved God and there were people who didn't know much about Him. There were people who thought they were good, but really weren't. All kinds of people came to hear Jesus.

One day when He was talking to the people, some scribes and Pharisees criticized Him. The scribes were called this because they copied the Old Testament (there were no printing presses then) and they thought that they knew all that God had to say to the people. The Pharisees were people who tried so hard to obey all of the laws in the Old Testament that they didn't have time to do kind deeds or to love God!

"Look at Him," they said. "He claims to be the Son of God. If He really is, why is He eating and talking to people who do such bad things?"

Jesus knew what the scribes and the Pharisees were saying. He knew that it was hard for them to understand why He did the things He did, so He told them stories to help them to understand.

One of the stories was about a lost sheep.

"A shepherd had a hundred sheep," He said. "Several times every day he counted them to be sure they were all there. One—two—three—four—five—six—all of the way to one hundred. One day when he counted his sheep, he found that there were only 99. One of the sheep was missing!

"The shepherd was sorry that the one little sheep was lost. He knew that it would die or get killed if he didn't find it. It wouldn't know where to find good green grass to eat. It might drown if it tried to drink from a swift river or a bear or lion might jump it and kill it.

"He was glad his 99 sheep were with him, but he felt bad for the one little lost sheep.

"There was only one thing to do. He had to go look for it. First, the shepherd saw that the 99 sheep were safe. Then he left them and went out to hunt for the lonely little lost sheep.

"He hunted and hunted. At last he found it, all alone and frightened. He ran to pick it up. He patted him and loved him. Then he put him over his shoulders and carried him back to where the other sheep were waiting. The shepherd was happy to have his sheep again, and when he got home he told all of his neighbors about finding his lost sheep. Oh! That shepherd was happy all right, just like the angels in heaven are happy when one lost person turns to God!"

Jesus told another story to the scribes and Pharisees to try to help them understand why God wanted Him to talk with people who were sinners and did bad things. This story is called "The Lost Coin."

"A woman had ten pieces of silver. She was very glad she had this money. She could buy many things with it, but she didn't want to spend it. She just liked to think about the things she could buy with it. Every day she'd count the money. One—two—three—four—five—six—seven—eight—nine—ten. Yes, it was all there.

"One day when she counted her money, there were only nine coins! Somehow, one had been lost!

"Do you think she was satisfied that she still had nine coins? No, indeed. She wanted all ten of them! She put her nine pieces of silver away. Then she got to work. She hunted everywhere. Then she got out her broom and very carefully swept the floor. She still didn't find the lost coin. She swept the floor again. This time she swept so carefully that she didn't miss a single inch. And sure enough! There was her piece of silver!

"The woman was very happy. She was so happy she wanted to tell everybody. She ran next door and called to her neighbors, 'I've found my coin! Be happy with me because my coin was lost, but now it is found!'"

Jesus told the people, "It's like that in heaven. When one person who does not know about God comes to Him, all the angels in heaven are happy!"

PROGRAM 17
LOVING OTHERS

Larger Scripture Lesson: Exodus 3 and 4

Scripture for Children's Church: Exodus 3:2-6

Object Lesson:

Love Your Brother

Object: Two brothers or two sisters, or a picture of two children

Some boys and girls are what is called an "only child." This means they don't have any brothers or sisters. Sometimes children like this get lonely. Maybe you are an only child. If you are, you probably know what I mean.

When we do have brothers or sisters, or both, we should be glad that we have them. Besides keeping each other company, brothers and sisters love each other. They don't always agree on everything, but that doesn't keep them from loving each other. Brothers and sisters are pretty special people, and we should be grateful for them. We should help them and work and play with them.

If you are lucky enough to have a brother or sister, always remember that they are very special people and God has been good to you by giving them to you. Your best friend can be your brother or your sister.

Application Story:

Andy's Big Brother

Andy slid into second base just as he heard the thud of the ball in the baseman's mitt. His knee stung where he had skinned it and the dirt hadn't settled yet, but he felt the base firmly beside his shoe. He waited tensely to hear the ump's decision.

"You're out!" the umpire shouted.

Oh, no! Not again! Hot tears stung his eyelids as he headed back toward his team's bench. The tears embarrassed him more than making the out. He didn't want any of the guys to think he was a sissy. It was bad enough to be a second-rate ball player.

"That's okay, Andy," he heard his coach say. "You did a really good job." "Come on, gang, let's get going!", he called to the other players.

The other fellows on the team didn't have much to say. They were all busy trying to do a good job themselves. Andy looked over at Eddy. "Eddy would have made it," he thought. "Eddy always made it. Why can't I do something right once in a while?" Andy watched his older brother shake his bright red hair back out of his face. He knew he looked like Ed, because his hair was red, too, and they both had freckles and blue eyes, but the similarity ended there. Andy was 15 months younger than Ed, and he was at least three inches shorter. Ed looked big and strong and healthy, but Andy was short and scrawny and puny. Besides being a better ball player, Ed made better grades than Andy did, too. "It's really tough to follow a brother like him," Andy thought. "Everybody expects so much of you. It just isn't fair."

Andy was roused from his thinking by the shouting from the bleachers. His father's voice rang out above the others'. "Atta boy, Eddy," he yelled.

Andy looked out at the field and saw that Ed, as usual, had made a good contact and had hit a three-bagger. He'd knocked Steve and Hal in and now the score was tied.

The next batter was out at first base but Eddy made it home to win the game by one run. Andy watched as he saw all of the boys on the team run to Ed and slap him on the back. "Great work, Ed! We did it again!", they yelled. They were pretty happy about winning this game because it put them in line for the championship. Andy was glad they'd won, but he wished he'd helped the team more.

"Come on, Andy," Ed called as he headed toward the place where their folks had told them they would meet them after the game. "Beat you to the car."

The two boys raced and, as usual, Ed won.

In school the next day Andy made a 90% on his spelling test. "That's very good, Andy," Miss Gray, his teacher, said. "But let's see if you can't do better next time. Eddy always made 100% when he was in my class."

"Yes'm," Andy answered. He was quiet on the outside, but on the inside he was boiling. "I get so tired of having everybody compare me to Eddy," he raged. "Why can't they just let me be *me?*"

After school, Andy waited for his brother because they always walked home together, but Eddy didn't come so he decided to go on alone. "Guess he had to stay after school for something," Andy thought, starting toward home without him.

As he drew near to their white stucco house, Andy noticed something strange going on. Neighbors were standing around in bunches on their front lawn and talking to each other. "That's funny," he thought, and then he heard the piercing siren of an approaching ambulance. He saw the ambulance stop in front of his own house!

He dashed up the terrace stairs and inside. The door was open and he heard voices in the front room. "He'll be all right, Mrs. Brown," he heard Dr. Cox say. "Just as soon as we get the results of the x-rays I'll let you know what they show."

"Mom, what's wrong?" Andy gasped as he burst into the living room.

"It's Eddy, Andy. He came home from school early today complaining from a pain in his side. He's very sick. They're not sure what it is, so Dr. Cox said we'd better get him to the hospital as quickly as possible. He thinks it may be his appendix."

Andy ran to the room that he shared with Eddy. Eddy was lying on his bed. "He must be awfully sick," Andy thought. His brown freckles stood out bold on his pale face and his eyes were closed. He opened them when he heard Andy come into the room. "I guess I won't be able to play the championship game tomorrow," he said softly. "But you'll win it for them, Andy."

Andy couldn't think of any old baseball game now. All he could think about was Ed. He didn't like to see him sick like this. He nodded his head dumbly because he couldn't think of anything to say. Besides, the lump in his throat was too big to talk. He watched as the attendants put his brother on the cart and carried him to the ambulance. After they had gone, Andy went back to his room and knelt beside his bed. He put his head on his folded arms. "Dear God," he prayed, "please take care of Eddy. He's my brother. Please don't let him die." He didn't try to hold his tears back now. They rolled down his cheeks and onto the bed. "And please, God, forgive me for not being a better brother. He can't help it because he's bigger and smarter and stronger than I am."

Andy got up from his knees and crawled onto the bed. He looked around the room. Everything reminded him of Ed. The rumpled bed beside his was just as it was when they took Eddy out of it. His baseball bat was propped up in the corner. His catcher's mitt was on the desk, with a baseball nestled in its grasp. The model planes they had assembled together were all lined up on the wall shelves. Eddy drifted off into sleep.

The house seemed very quiet when he awoke. It was dark outside. "I must have slept a long time," he thought. And then he remembered Eddy. "How old was he?" He dashed down the steps two at a time and met his dad on the landing.

"Hi, Son! I was just coming to get you," he said as he put his arm around Andy's shoulder. "Eddy wanted me to tell you hello for him. The x-rays verified what Dr. Cox suspected and they are operating right now. I came home to get you so we both could go back and be with your mother. We knew you'd want to be there, too."

"How is he?" Andy asked. "Does he hurt awfully bad?"

"They've given him medicine to relieve the pain, so he felt much better. But Dr. Cox felt that it was better to get that appendix out before it burst."

Andy and his father went out to the car and drove to the hospital. It didn't take long, and soon they had joined Mrs. Brown in the waiting room on the top floor of the hospital.

"Any news yet?" Mr. Brown asked.

"No, none," his wife answered as she shook her head.

The three of them sat down on the brown leather chairs and settled back. They knew it would take a while, but each time a nurse or a doctor walked by they looked up expectantly. No one offered any news about Eddy. It seemed as though they sat there for hours. Andy looked at the big round clock on the white wall. The slight hum of its electric motor sounded loud in the quiet corridor. He watched the minute hand as it slowly moved around the black numbers. Now it was 11 o'clock. What a long evening it had been. Andy wished Dr. Cox would come.

Mr. and Mrs. Brown and Andy all turned when they heard Dr. Cox's padded footsteps down the hall. Andy couldn't tell if he had good news or bad from the look on his face. Now that he was going to hear about Eddy, he was scared. Then he wished Dr. Cox would hurry up and say something.

Finally, the doctor came to a halt before the waiting trio. He slowly shook his head. He looked tired. "It has been a very serious operation, but we think Eddy is going to be all right. It will be a long time before he is strong again. He is still sleeping, but you can look in on him for a minute before you go home."

Mr. and Mrs. Brown and Andy followed Dr. Cox to Eddy's room. Eddy looked terribly thin and pale lying there in the **stark white bed.** He had a needle in his arm connected to a long hose hanging from a bottle on a stand. Andy thought Eddy looked awfully sick. "I hope Dr. Cox is right," he thought. "I hope Eddy is really all right."

Soon Andy and his parents were on their way home. Mr. Brown parked the car and they went into the house. Andy took **his bath and got into** his pajamas. He was very tired, but he remembered to slide to his knees before he got into bed.

"Dear God," he prayed. "Thank you for taking care of **Eddy.** Thank you for helping Dr. Cox to operate on him. Dr. Cox said Eddy'd be weak for a while, so help me to be a good little brother to him for a while. He's always been a good big brother to me! Thank you. Amen."

Just before he turned the light off, Andy opened his Bible. He turned to a verse in the book of Hebrews and read: "Let brotherly love continue" (Hebrews 13:1).

"Let brotherly love continue," he murmured. "That's a good verse. Even God thinks brothers are pretty special people to each other. I'm glad I have one."

Andy turned off the lamp and pulled his covers up over his shoulders. "I'll play a good ball game for Eddy tomorrow," he thought. "We've got to win that game for him 'cause he's a real **champ.**"

Bible Story:

Moses And The Burning Bush

Moses was a shepherd. Every day he went out into the desert and watched the sheep. Sometimes he stayed all night, too. He was a shepherd long before David, but he must have thought about some of the things that David thought about.

He must have looked all around him at the vast land and thought about God. He must have looked up at the clear blue sky and the fluffy white clouds and thought about God. He must have wondered at God's great power to create the world and the skies and all that are in them. He must have felt very close to God while he was out there all alone in the desert with the sheep.

One day while Moses was watching the sheep on the mountain

97

called Horeb, he saw a very strange sight. He saw a great big bush on fire. He walked closer to the bush. The flames were bright red and orange. He could feel the heat from them. "How did it start?" Moses wondered. "And why doesn't the bush burn up?" He watched and watched. The bush burned and burned. The land was dry and the other bushes were dry, and if it had been an ordinary fire, the whole countryside would have been in flames by now. But the bush continued to burn. And nothing else caught fire because of it. Flames leaped high into the air.

While he was wondering and watching, Moses heard a voice. "Moses! Moses!"

"Here I am," he answered, wondering who it was who was calling him.

The voice from the bush said, "Do not come closer. You are standing on holy ground. Take off your shoes."

Moses bent down and slipped his sandals off his feet.

The voice went on. "I am the God of your father, the God of Abraham and Isaac and Jacob."

Moses put his hands over his face because he was afraid to look at God.

God continued to talk. "I know that my people, the Israelites, are in serious trouble. I know they are treated badly and are slaves of the Egyptians. I have heard their cries and I have now come to help them. I want you to go to Egypt and to the Pharoah and bring my people out of Egypt."

"Who am I to do this?" Moses asked God.

"I will be with you," God said. "I promise you that you will bring my people here to this mountain to worship Me."

"But," Moses argued, "when I go to the Israelites and tell them You sent me, what if they ask me Your name? What shall I tell them?"

"Tell them Jehovah God has sent you. Tell them that God the Creator of all things has sent you. Tell them that the God of Abraham and Isaac and Jacob has sent you. Go," God said, "and gather all of the leaders of Israel, and tell them that I have visited you and have told you that I have heard their prayers."

God continued. "Tell them that I will rescue them from slavery and lead them to a land where there is plenty of good things to eat."

"The leaders will listen to you," God said. "I want you to take them to the Pharoah. Tell him also that I have spoken to you. Tell him that you want him to allow the Israelites to go into the wilderness to worship Me. He won't let you go, but I will stretch out my mighty hand and will allow much trouble to come to the Egyptians until they do let my people go."

"But they will not believe me," Moses argued. "They won't believe that you have come to me."

The Lord said, "Take that rod in your hand and throw it to the ground."

Moses did what God told him to do. He threw his rod to the ground. The rod became a big snake and Moses was afraid of it. He started to run away.

But God said, "Put your hand out and take it by the tail."

Moses very carefully put out his hand and grabbed the snake by its tail. Just as soon as he had done this, it was no longer a snake. The snake had turned back into his rod again.

"Now," God said, "put your hand inside your coat."

Moses put his hand in his coat and then pulled it out. He gasped. It was white and full of sores. He had leprosy!

"Now, put your hand back inside your coat and take it out again," God instructed.

Moses put his hand back inside his coat. He took it out again very slowly. Moses was very happy to see that his hand was all well again.

"And if they don't believe these two signs and still won't listen to you, take some water out of the river and pour it upon the dry land. When you pour it out, the water will turn into blood."

"But, Lord, I am not a good speaker," Moses said.

"Who made man's mouth?", God asked Moses. "Don't you think I can handle that problem? Do as I say and I will be your mouth and teach you what to say."

"Oh, Lord, send someone to help me," Moses begged.

God wasn't happy with Moses because this showed that he didn't have faith in Him, but He said, "I shall have your brother Aaron to help you then. I will tell you what I want done, you will tell Aaron, and then Aaron will tell the people."

As soon as God had stopped talking to Moses, the bush was no longer in flames. It stood dry and brittle just as it had been. Moses knew that God had spoken to him. Now he had to do what God had told him to do.

He sat down and put on his sandals. "This truly is holy ground," he said, "because God Himself was here.

PROGRAM 18
CHOOSING THE RIGHT WAY

Larger Scripture Lesson: Matthew 4:1-11
Scripture for Children's Church: Matthew 4:1, 2
Object Lesson:

Doing Things The Right Way

Object: A dictionary

It's wonderful to be able to read. We look forward to learning how as soon as we get in the first grade. We start out with easy words. Then the words get harder and harder until finally we start reading words we don't even understand! When this happens, there are three things we can do:

1. We can completely ignore the word and just skip over it.
2. We can try to figure it out by ourselves.
3. We can go to a dictionary and find out what it means.

If we ignore the word altogether, we might not be able to understand what we are reading at all.

If we try to figure out what it means, we may do it wrong. Then we won't be sure of what we are reading.

But if we look the word up and find out what it means, we not only understand what we are reading, but we have learned a new word.

There is a right way to do things and a wrong way.

The right way to read is to look up words in the dictionary when we don't know what they mean.

Application Story:

Left At The Park

Harry piled into the car with the other boys and girls. They didn't mind being crowded. It was all part of the fun.

"Say, Mr. Green, it's awfully nice of you to take us on this picnic. This is fun! How long are we going to stay?" Harry asked.

Mr. Green looked at his watch while the last of the children squeezed in and pulled the door shut. "It's 12:15 now," he said. "We'll probably leave around 3:00. Let's see now. Who all do we have? Jerry, Mickey, Tom, Jim, Mary, George, Jean, and Harry. That makes eight of you. All of you remember to keep track of me and each other so everyone will get home safely. When we get to the park, it will be easy to get mixed up with all of the other people."

He turned on the ignition and released the brake. "Okay!" he said. "Let's go!"

It took about half an hour to get to the park where all the other Sunday School boys and girls had gone with their teachers. They were all ready to jump out of the car as soon as they got there.

"That must be our shelter house," George yelled, pointing toward some people he knew who were putting food on some tables.

"I'll beat you all over there," Harry shouted. The boys all raced to the shelter house, but they soon scattered as they joined the other groups who were playing ball or sliding down the slides.

Harry and George were among the first in line when Mr. Brewster, the Sunday School superintendent, rang the dinner bell. The paper plates were soon stacked with salads and fried chicken, and the boys found seats at one of the long tables.

"Boy! This sure is good!" Harry said as he chewed on a chicken leg. "I wish we'd do this every Saturday!"

"Yeah," George answered. "What're you going to do after we eat?"

"I don't know. I was thinking about going exploring in the woods. Want to go with me?"

"Not me, "George said. "We might get lost."

"Oh, no we won't. I go exploring in my Grandpa's woods all of the time. Come on. Don't be a piker!"

"Well, all right. But just a little way," George finally agreed.

After their plates were cleaned up, the two boys each took an apple and headed toward the woods. The trees weren't very close together at first, but it wasn't long until they became dense.

George stopped. "This is as far as I'm going," he told Harry.

"Well, okay. Go on back," Harry told him. "But I'm not going to."

George headed back toward the shelter house and Harry went

deeper into the woods. It got darker and darker because the leaves of the trees hid the sun. Still Harry went on.

"Wouldn't it be funny if they thought I was lost," he thought. "I think I'll just stay here until someone comes after me." He looked at his wristwatch. It was 2:45. "They'll be leaving shortly. I think I'll just sit on this log and wait."

He waited until 3 o'clock. No one had come to find him yet. He waited until 3:15. Still no one came. Finally, tired from the walk and the waiting, Harry leaned his head back on a tree trunk and went fast asleep.

An hour later, Harry awoke with a start. "Where in the world am I," he wondered. And then he remembered. "What time is it now?" He looked at his watch. "Wow! It is 4:15. I wonder where everybody is? I'd better go find out."

Harry ran back through the trees. It was darker now than it had been when he'd come. When he reached the edge of the woods, he looked toward the shelterhouse where his group had eaten. It was all cleaned up, and there wasn't a person in it! They had all gone home without him!

Harry hadn't been afraid in the woods, but he didn't feel as brave now. "I guess this is what I get for being so dumb," he thought. "It's my own fault, but who'd have thought they'd have gone off and left me?"

He sat down on an empty bench. "I'd better decide what I'm going to do," he thought. "But I guess there's no deciding. It looks like there's only one way for me to get back home and that's to walk. I might as well get started," he sighed.

Soon he was walking through the park to the street. "Lucky I know how to get home from here," he thought. "It takes a half an hour to drive it, so I should be home in a couple of hours if I hurry."

"Beep! Beep!" Harry turned to see who was honking at him. Why, it was Mr. Green!

"Oh, boy, am I glad to see you!" Harry said as he ran over to the car.

"Well, I'm pretty happy to see you, too," Mr. Green said with a grin. "I thought you'd gone back with someone else when we left because you were nowhere in sight. When we got almost home George told me about how you two had gone off into the woods. I wish you hadn't done that, Harry. You gave me quite a scare!"

"I'm sorry, Mr. Green. Really, I guess I was kind of scared, too. I'm sorry I didn't do like I was told!"

"Well, Harry, it's all right this time," Mr. Green said, "but if it happens any more, people will feel like they can't depend upon you. You don't want that to happen, do you?"

"No, Sir," Harry answered. "I won't do it again. Next time maybe there won't be a Mr. Green who'll come back for me!"

Bible Story:

Jesus Chose The Right Way

After Jesus was baptized, He walked out into the wilderness. He stayed out there for forty days and forty nights with nothing to eat or drink. Satan tried to tempt Him and make Him sin, but Jesus always chose the right way. He didn't sin one time during His whole lifetime. This doesn't mean that he *couldn't* sin, it means that He chose *not* to sin or to do anything wrong.

The Bible tells us that there were at least three things that Satan tried to get Jesus to do while He was out in the wilderness.

"Prove that You are the Son of God," Satan said. "You are hungry. You need food. Command these stones to turn into bread. If you really are the Son of God, You can do it."

Jesus looked at the stones. He thought, "I am the Son of God, but I don't have to prove it to Satan. I am hungry, but that is not why I am here on earth. I am here to save the people from their sins, not to satisfy my own hunger."

He said to Satan, "I could do it. But that is not what is important. It is the Word of God that is important."

Satan failed the first time, but he did not give up. He took Jesus to Jerusalem and set Him high on the temple.

"If You are the Son of God," Satan said, "throw Yourself down, because you won't get hurt. The Bible says that God's angels will take care of You."

Jesus looked down. There were many people below. If He threw Himself down like Satan said, He knew that the people would see Him and make Him their King immediately.

But He said, "You should not try to test God."

Satan had failed the second time, but he still did not give up. He took Jesus to the top of a very high mountain.

"Look at all of that," he said, pointing toward all of the land in every direction. "If You will bow down and worship me, I will give You all of these kingdoms for Your very Own."

Jesus said, "Go away. God says that there is only one God and He only should be worshiped."

Then Satan left Jesus. He had done all he could to tempt Jesus, for the time being anyway. He did not want Jesus to do what God had sent Him to do. He wanted to keep Jesus from being perfect. He knew that if Jesus had done any of the things that he had suggested that He would not have been perfect. Then Jesus would not have had the power to overcome death and Satan. And, if Jesus could not overcome death, we could not overcome it through Him.

Jesus was true to God. He didn't sin because He knew God did not want Him to sin.

Aren't you glad that He chose to do the right thing? He is our example. If we really love Him, we will always try to be like Him.

PROGRAM 19
MAKING FRIENDS

Larger Scripture Lesson: Daniel 1

Scripture for Children's Church: Daniel 1:3-5

Object Lesson:

People Are Like Apples!

Object: An apple

Choosing your friends is very important. Of course, you wouldn't want to choose certain people to be your friends just because of the good things they could do for you, but you do want to be careful to have friends who help you to do the things that are right.

If you had a bushel of apples and all of the apples were good except one, the good apples would never make the bad apple good. It's always the other way around. The bad apple would make the good ones bad.

It really shouldn't be that way with people, but it is. A good person should be able to help his bad friends become better people, but more than likely it works the other way around. The people who do bad things usually get the good people to go along with them. That is why it is so important to make friends with people who do things that are right.

Application Story:

A Trip To The Principal's Office

The seventh-grade messenger handed a note to Miss Donovan. With a serious look on her face, she read it and said, "Eddie James and Luther Jones, you are wanted in the principal's office. He wants you both right away."

Eddie's heart did a flip flop. "Why did Mr. England want him and Luther? Boy, what have we done wrong," he wondered. He couldn't remember any trouble they had been in, but he knew that they must have done something. Mr. England didn't call people to the office often, but when he did, it was usually because of trouble.

Eddie slowly closed the book he was reading and followed his best friend, Luther, out of the room.

Some people thought that it was strange that Eddie and Luther were best friends because Eddie was white and Luther was colored. The two boys didn't see what was so strange about it though. They both liked the same things and were the same size and the same age. Most important of all, they liked each other.

Eddie didn't have any brothers or sisters, but Luther had three of each—three brothers and three sisters. Eddie liked to go to Luther's house because they always seemed to have so much fun over there. Being different colors didn't make any difference to them.

As soon as they got outside the room, the two puzzled boys turned toward each other. "Boy! What do you think Mr. England wants?" Eddie wondered out loud.

"I don't have any ideas," Luther answered. "But it's sure to be some kind of trouble."

Slowly the two boys walked down the steps to the school office on the first floor. Slowly they opened the office door and walked up to the secretary's desk.

"Mr. England wants to see us," Eddie told the lady sitting at the desk.

"Please have a chair, boys. I'll tell Mr. England you're here," she told them.

Eddie and Luther backed up to two of the chairs that were lined up against one of the walls. They didn't say a word to each other. Eddie knew Luther was just as scared as he was.

Eddie could hear the low rumble of two men talking in Mr. England's office, even though the door between them was closed. He tried very hard to understand what they were saying, but he couldn't make out the words. His blond head leaned forward as he listened. His body was tense and stiff. Were they talking about him and Luther? Who could the strange man be?

Eddie looked at Luther. "He's trying to understand what they're saying, too," he thought. But he could tell by the expression on Luther's shiny brown face that his friend was just as puzzled as Eddie himself was.

Both boys jumped when the phone on the secretary's desk buzzed. "Yes, Mr. England, they're here. I'll send them right in."

When she hung up the receiver she looked at them. "You may go into Mr. England's office now," she said.

Eddie and Luther steeled themselves for whatever might happen inside that room. They looked at each other again. "No matter what happens, I'm glad we're here together," Luther whispered.

"Me, too," Eddie answered. "Come on. Let's get it over with."

The door to Mr. England's office swung open, and Mr. England stepped into the doorway.

"Hello, Eddie and Luther," he said. "Come right in."

The boys walked into the principal's private office and the door shut behind them.

"You boys know Mr. Williams. He owns the candy store across the street from the school."

The boys nodded. Yes, they knew Mr. Williams. He was a nice old man who liked kids. "What did Mr. Williams want with them," Eddie wondered.

"Have a seat, boys," Mr. England invited. "Mr. Williams has come here to check on you two. He says he has been very busy in his store at noon time and has been wondering about hiring one of you to help him out."

The elderly storekeeper smiled at Eddie and Luther. They smiled back. What a relief! Eddie began to relax and he heard Luther heave a big sigh.

Mr. England continued. "I have told Mr. Williams that both of you boys have fine records. Now our problem seems to be which one of yo ushould help in the store."

Eddie thought that working in the store would be great fun. He didn't know how Luther felt, of course, but he'd probably like to do it, too.

"Well, Boys, which one of you wants to work for Mr. Williams? He'll pay a dollar a day for one of you."

"I'd like to," Eddie and Luther both said at the same time.

"Well, now that's our problem. He only needs one boy. We thought maybe you two could help us decide which one."

"I think Eddie should have it, Sir," Luther said.

"Well, I'd like to do it all right, because it would be lots of fun," Eddie agreed. "But Luther really needs it more than I do. He's got a big family at his house, and I'm sure they need the money."

"But Eddie's my friend," Luther argued. "I don't want to take the job away from him."

"I think Eddie has a point, though, Luther," Mr. England

said. "We hadn't really considered the money angle, and it is a very important one. Your folks would probably appreciate the help it would give them."

Mr. Williams scratched his head as he thought.

"I know what we can do," he said. "Why don't we give Luther the noon job. And then both of you can come in a couple of hours on Saturday mornings and clean up the shop?"

"Oh, that's great!" Eddie agreed. "How about that, Luther?"

Luther's big brown eyes sparkled. "If it's okay with you, Eddie, it sure is with me!" he said. "When do you want us to start, Mr. Williams?"

"How about tomorrow, Luther? And then I'll see you Saturday, Eddie. Is that all right?"

The two friends grinned at each other. Here they had come to Mr. England's office expecting trouble, and they had ended up getting jobs instead!

"I'll say it is!" Luther said.

"Thanks, Mr. Williams," Eddie added. "This is great!"

"Well, if everything is settled, you may go back to class, now," Mr. England suggested.

"Yes, Sir!"

"Thank you, Sir!"

Eddie and Luther left the office.

When they got into the hall, they stopped and turned to each other.

"Boy! What a relief!" they both said at the same time, laughing hard.

"Thanks for offering me the job first," Eddie said. "You're a real friend. When a guy has a friend like you, he's pretty lucky."

"I think you're a good friend, too," Luther answered.

The two boys put their arms around each other's shoulders and happily headed for class. Eddie gave Luther's shoulder a little squeeze. "Wait'll we tell the rest of the kids," he said. "Won't they be surprised!"

Bible Story:

Daniel And His Friends

Daniel was a prince in Judah. He was a young man, handsome and rich. Daniel spent the first years of his life in his own home, but something dreadful happened to him and to his family, and, in fact, to everyone in his country.

Soldiers from Babylon came and fought them. Many, many people were killed. Before the soldiers left Babylon, King Nebuchadnezzar gave an order to the man in charge. He said, "Bring some of the princes back. Be sure they are young men who are healthy and smart. After three years, bring them to me and I will look them over."

So Daniel and some other young princes had been captured and taken to Babylon. Here, the Babylonians treated them very well. They gave them a good place to stay and good food to eat. In fact, they gave the young men the same food that the king himself ate.

However, Daniel and three of his friends, Shadrach, Meshach, and Abednego, decided that they should not eat such rich, fancy food because it was not good for them. Daniel and his friends knew that their bodies belonged to God and that they should take good care of them. Daniel said, "This food is too rich for us. We won't be strong and healthy if we eat it."

"I am afraid to disobey the king," the servant said. "He has ordered that you all eat the same things that he eats. If you should look worse than the others when he sees you, he will kill me."

"Try it and see," Daniel said. "Give us vegetables and water for ten days. If we don't look better than the others by then, do what you will with us."

"All right. We'll try it for ten days," the head servant said to Daniel.

All the other princes ate the rich food and drank wine, but for ten days Daniel, Shadrach, Meshach, and Abednego ate only vegetables and drank only water. When the head servant came to check on them, he agreed with Daniel that they did look better and healthier than the others. "You are right," he said. "You may have your own way and eat only vegetables and drink only water."

While the princes were in captivity, King Nebuchadnezzar gave them teachers. These wise men taught them many things.

After three years, King Nebuchadnezzar said, "It is time for me to see the young princes that we captured in Judah. Bring them to me."

Daniel, Shadrach, Meshach, and Abednego and all the other princes came in to the large beautiful room where the king was waiting for them.

The king asked them many questions and talked to them for a long time. He was surprised that the young men were so smart.

He discovered that Daniel, Shadrach, Meshach, and Abednego were not only healthier than the others, they were also smarter. They were even smarter than the wise men who had taught them!

Daniel, Shadrach, Meshach, and Abednego were glad that they were friends. They all knew that it helped to have friends who did the right thing. It's always easier to do the right thing if you have friends who are doing it. It is always wise to choose friends who will help you to be a better person.

PROGRAM 20
MAKING FRIENDS

Larger Scripture Lesson: I Samuel 17:17-20:42
Scripture for Children's Church: I Samuel 20:18-23
Object Lesson:

How To Have Friends

Object: Two boys or two girls who are close friends.

I have asked _____ and _____ to come up here
to stand with me because they are something special to each
other. Can anybody guess what? (Give opportunity for answers).
Yes, they are friends.

How do you know they are friends? You know because they
like to be together, for one thing. They are kind to one another,
too. They share with each other. They like each other. (Let the
children sit down.)

It is good to have friends. Friends help us when we are in
trouble. They keep us company when we are lonely.

It is also good to be a friend. If we want to be a friend, we
must help people when they need help. We will be kind to them.
We won't fuss and argue with them. We will share with them.

If we want to have friends, we must be willing to be a friend.
Application Story:

Eleanor Helps Her Helper!

The fourth grade class of Whittier School swooshed into the
classroom like water pouring from a fire hydrant. The boys and
girls swirled in and out the rows. Perspiring and breathless, their
heated bodies and tousled heads began to take order as they
found their places.

Slowly, one by one, their attention was drawn to a new student
sitting at a desk which had been empty before they had gone

out to the playground. Silently and carefully they evaluated their new classmate.

Helen, who found herself sitting beside the new girl, looked her over openly. "Look at her," she thought. "Thinks she's smart. Looks conceited to me. Well, I'm not going to like *her*!"

Frances, sitting behind the new girl, eyed her suspiciously. "She's pretty. But rather stuck up, I'd guess," she thought.

Eleanor was neither conceited nor stuck up. At the moment, she was a very frightened young lady dreading the introduction which she knew would not be long in coming.

Miss Smith clapped her hands for attention. Everyone stopped gawking and turned to face the teacher. Eleanor sighed from relief. She had hated the looking over she had gotten. But then she remembered. "Here it comes," she thought. "Now Miss Smith is going to introduce me. I hope I don't have to stand up."

"Children, as you see, we have someone new in our class today," Miss Smith said. "Her name is Eleanor Murphy. Eleanor has just arrived from Ponca City, Oklahoma. Her father is Reverend Murphy, the new preacher. I'm sure Eleanor and you will all become good friends. Helen, I'd like to ask you to be Eleanor's helper for several days. She will need someone to show her around for a while."

"Now," Miss Smith said as she began to pass out long narrow sheets of paper, "will you please clear your desks. We are going to have a spelling test."

"Oh, my," Eleanor thought, "I hope I know the words!"

One by one the boys and girls wrote the words on their papers as Miss Smith called them out. Eleanor became a little more confident. The words were not new. She had been working on them before she left the school in Ponca City.

"All right, children, please pass your papers to the person on your right to be graded. You who are in the last row may take yours over to the children on the other side of the room."

Eleanor smiled timidly as she passed her paper over to Helen. Helen took the paper. Her sour expression indicated that she had no intentions of smiling at Eleanor. "And she's been assigned to stay with me for at least two days," Eleanor thought as she sat back in her seat. She wished she wasn't here at this old school. She wished she was back in Ponca City.

After the papers were graded, Helen passed Eleanor's back to her. Eleanor glanced gratefully at the 100% on it, but her pleasure died when she heard Helen whisper, "Think you're smart, don't you?"

After the arithmetic lesson, Miss Smith dismissed the class for lunch. Everyone rose from his seat and headed for the door. That is, everyone except Eleanor. She didn't know where to go. Wondering what she should do, she heard Helen say, "Well, come on." She was glad Helen had remembered her.

"Thanks," Eleanor said, "I don't know where the lunch-room is."

"Miss Smith said I had to show you around, so I guess I'll have to. Don't be so pokey," Helen said as she turned to follow her classmates.

After lunch, Eleanor and Helen went out on the playground. They walked over to the hopscotch game painted in white lines on the asphalt pavement. Eleanor felt sorry that Helen had to stay with her because Miss Smith had told her to, but she was glad she didn't have to be left alone. It was terrible having to leave all your old friends to come to a brand new school. Daddy had said it was "God's will" for him to accept the new pastorate. "I wonder if it's God's will that I come here to Whittier," she thought. "I hope He takes care of me like Daddy says He takes care of him!"

Gradually, Helen began to be a little more friendly, but not much. The bell rang and classes began again. After school Eleanor was happy to go home at last. It had been a long day.

Friday dawned clear and cool. Eleanor reached school right on time. She didn't want to have to stand around alone before the bell rang. She was glad some of the girls and boys in her class spoke to her when she came into the room. She wished Helen would, but Helen seemed to be too busy getting books out of her desk to notice her.

At noon Helen reluctantly waited for Eleanor again.

"Come on," she said. "The other kids will get ahead of us."

Eleanor hurried as fast as she could. She noticed that Helen shoved the younger boys and girls out of the way. "Maybe it's not just me she doesn't like," she thought. "It doesn't seem like she cares about anybody."

Out on the playground after lunch, the two girls headed for the hopscotch corner. Someone was already using it.

"This is our place," Helen said. "We were here yesterday."

"That's too bad. We're here today," Frances, one of the other girls, answered.

"Oh, yeah? Well, we're going to be here today ourselves," Helen said as she shoved Frances.

"Yeah?" Frances answered, giving Helen an even harder shove.

Push. Push. Back and forth they pushed. Finally, Helen pushed so hard that she knocked Frances down.

"Wait! Wait!" Eleanor cried out. She pointed toward another corner. "There's an empty hopscotch over there. Let's use it, Helen."

"Well, okay," Helen said reluctantly.

The two girls walked away.

"Why didn't you help me?" Helen complained. "It was your hopscotch, too."

"I guess I didn't think it was right to take it away from them. They were there first."

"You don't fight much, do you?" Helen asked.

"Well, I try not to. Jesus doesn't want us to fight. He wants us to be peacemakers."

"Who's Jesus?" Helen asked.

"Why, Jesus is God's Son. He died on the cross for our sins and rose again. Do you mean you haven't ever heard about Him?"

"Well, I've heard His name, all right. But I never knew who He was. How do you know?"

"I learn about Him in Sunday School and church. Why don't you go with me Sunday? My folks'd be glad to pick you up. You could go with me to my class."

"I don't know," Helen answered. "Mom always likes to sleep late on Sundays. But I guess I could set the alarm myself."

The school bell rang and classes began once again. Soon the afternoon had passed, and the boys and girls were dismissed.

When Eleanor reached the front door on her way out, she heard loud voices. Looking out at the crowd of children gathered in front of the school, she saw Helen and Frances in the center of it. It looked like they were going to fight again. Eleanor ran over to them.

"What's the matter?" she asked. "Can I help?"

Helen and Frances looked at her in amazement. No one had ever approached them like this before. They looked at each other. Helen sort of chuckled. Frances began to laugh, too. Eleanor looked so funny, standing there, with that comical look on her face, wanting to help! They both laughed and laughed. Finally, Helen said, "I guess you have already, Eleanor. I'm not mad any more!"

She turned to the other girl, "Sorry, Frances. Eleanor doesn't like for us to fight. She says that Jesus doesn't think it's good either."

Frances looked sheepish. "I know it isn't. But sometimes I forget. It's so easy to do it, though, isn't it?"

"Maybe we both need to know more about this Jesus. Why don't you go with us to Sunday School Sunday?" Helen asked.

"I guess it wouldn't hurt me any," Frances answered. "Yeah. Why not?"

"My folks'll pick you up, too, if you'd like," Eleanor offered.

"No, thanks. I don't live too far from the church. Didn't Miss Smith say that your dad is the preacher? It should be fun listening to somebody's father. What time does it start?"

"At 9:30."

"Okay, I'll see you there!"

The crowd of boys and girls broke up and headed for home. Eleanor skipped along with a happy heart. Her first two days at school had turned out just fine. And now she even knows someone in Sunday School, too! She was glad that she and Helen were friends now. And Frances, too. It's nice to have friends. Jesus was right. We're much happier if we are peacemakers. Nobody makes anything from fighting; but, by *not* fighting, you make friends!

Bible Story:

Jonathan And David

Jonathan was the prince of Israel. David was a shepherd boy. Even though these two young men came from very different kinds of homes, they loved each other. They were what we sometimes call "best friends."

David had just killed the giant Goliath to save Israel from the Philistines. This great giant had made fun of the Israelite soldiers because none of them was brave enough to come out and fight him alone. Goliath had said that if he killed the Israelite soldier who challenged him, the Philistines would be the winners of the battle. But if the Israelite soldier killed him, the Israelites would be the victors.

David was visiting his brothers in the soldiers' camp when he heard Goliath.

"Why doesn't someone accept his challenge?" David asked. "God is on our side. Whoever fights for us will win. Why, I'd even do it myself, because I know that God would let me win."

When King Saul heard about this, he gave David permission to fight the giant Philistine.

David chose five smooth stones and his slingshot for weapons to fight against Goliath.

Almost before the giant knew what was happening, David had slung a stone from his slingshot. The stone hit Goliath on the forehead and he fell to the ground, unconscious. Then the young shepherd boy killed the giant with the giant's own sword.

Abner, the captain of the Israelite army, took David to King Saul and his son, Jonathan.

The king had known David before, because David had played his harp for Saul when he was sick, but evidently he didn't recognize him, because he said, "Who are you?"

"I am David, the son of Jesse of Bethlehem," David answered.

"I want you to stay here at the palace," King Saul commanded.

Prince Jonathan looked at David. David looked at Jonathan. Immediately they liked each other.

They talked together many times while David was living in the palace. They became the best of friends. In fact, to prove to David how much he loved him, Jonathan took off his beautiful robe one day and gave it to him. Then he took off his belt and gave it to him. He even gave him his bow and his sword.

David didn't have anything to give to Jonathan. But Jonathan knew that David loved him, too. The young men told each other that they would always love one another and take care of each other. If something should happen to one of them, they promised that the other would look after him and his children, if he had any.

King Saul made David a captain in his army and all of the soldiers under David liked him. King Saul's servants liked David, too. In fact, all of the Israelites liked him. They heard about how he had killed Goliath and they sang and danced in his honor.

King Saul became very jealous. He thought that everyone liked David better than they liked him. He got so jealous that he tried to get rid of David. He sent him out to fight hard battles, hoping that he would get killed, but God helped David and he didn't get hurt.

Prince Jonathan knew King Saul wanted to kill his friend. He did everything he could to prevent it. He talked to his father about David and tried to get him to stop, but Jonathan knew when King Saul got angry that he would do it anyway.

Sometimes King Saul had David play his harp for him. One day while David was playing, the king threw a javelin at him. The javelin missed David, and became embedded in the wall. David ran away.

He didn't know what to do, so he went to Jonathan.

"What have I done to make the king hate me so much?" he asked his friend.

"Don't worry, David. You won't die. God will protect you," Jonathan answered. "What can I do to help you?"

David and Jonathan made a plan. Jonathan was supposed to check to see if his father still wanted to kill David.

"Stay away for a while, David," he said. "On the third day come back here and hide behind this large rock. I will come and shoot three arrows out into the field. If my father is no longer angry, I will say to my servant, 'Behold, the arrows are on this side of you.' But, if my father still wants to kill you, I will tell the servant, 'Behold, the arrows are ahead of you.'"

The first day that David didn't come to the table, King Saul didn't think too much about it. But on the second night, when he didn't show up, the king said to Jonathan, "Where is David? He didn't come to the table yesterday and he is not here again today."

"He has gone to Bethlehem," Jonathan said. "I gave him permission to go."

King Saul became very angry. He shouted, "You are an ungrateful son. You know that if David lives that you will not be king after I die. Why do you take David's side against me?"

In his anger, King Saul threw a javelin at Jonathan, his own son, but he missed him.

Jonathan became angry, too. He was ashamed of his father. He got up and left the table.

The next morning Jonathan got out of bed and took his boy servant with him out to the field where he knew David would be waiting behind the rock.

"Run," Jonathan said. "Get the arrows which I will shoot."

While the boy was running, Jonathan pulled back on the string on his bow and let the arrow fly through the air.

"Is not the arrow beyond you?" Jonathan shouted.

David understood what Jonathan was telling him. Now he knew for sure that King Saul wanted to kill him.

When the boy had gathered all of Jonathan's arrows, he came back to his master. Jonathan gave him his bow and the rest of his arrows. "Carry these back to the city for me," Jonathan told him, and the boy left.

David came out from behind the rock. Jonathan and David threw their arms around each other and cried. The two friends knew that they would not be able to be together any more.

117

"Go," Jonathan said. "And remember the promises we have made to each other. God be with you."

David turned away from the city and Jonathan turned back toward the city. Each went his own way. Perhaps they would never see each other again, but they knew that no matter what happened they would always be friends.

PROGRAM 21
HELPING OTHERS

Larger Scripture Lesson: Mark 12:28-31; Luke 10:30-35
Scripture for Children's Church: Mark 12:28-31
Object Lesson:

Helping Our Parents

Object: Trash basket

Boys and girls are sometime unhappy when their mothers ask them to do things around the house. They fuss and make excuses and sometimes are not very nice about it. Mother has to tell them over and over what she wants them to do.

Are you ever like that? If you're like most boys and girls, you are.

God tells us in the Bible that we should obey our parents. He gave us our parents so they could take care of us and help us to learn what is right and wrong. And it is right to help other people.

God wants us to help our parents, too. There are a lot of ways that we can help them. We can empty the trash (show trash basket). We can empty the garbage. We can make our beds. We can keep our clothes picked up. Can you name some other ways you can help at your house? (Allow the children to name some ways they can help.)

Now that we know more ways to help, let's all show our parents that we love them by helping them. This will make them happy, and it will make you happy. It will make God happy, too.

Application Story:

Bert's Afternoon Sunday School

"Hurry up, Chuck!" Bert Higgins yelled at his friend, Chuck Peterson, when he reached his front yard. He gasped for air.

119

"Hi! Sorry I'm late, but I was reading a keen story in the library book I checked out yesterday."

The two boys trotted up the street together. A half a block from school, they broke into a run when they heard the hoarse buzz telling them it was time for classes to begin. They raced down the walk, up the steps, into the long corridor, and toward their room. They were just taking their seats when the tardy bell rang.

Bert winked at Chuck. They'd made it. At least they weren't late. He hadn't had time to talk to Chuck about going to church with him like he'd intended, though. "I'll have to do it tonight," he thought, "because this is Friday."

Chuck and Bert liked their classes. They liked to play ball even better. After school and a short game of scrub, they started home.

"Hey, Chuck, want to go to Sunday School with me Sunday? You'd like my teacher. He's swell."

Chuck shook his head. "I can't go anywhere on Saturday or Sunday. Mom has a weekend job at the hospital and I have to stay home with Gramps."

Bert knew that Chuck's grandfather had to sit in a wheelchair all day.

"Oh, yeah. I guess I forgot," he said.

Bert had just accepted Jesus as his Savior, and he knew Chuck was not a Christian. He wanted Chuck to come to Sunday School so he could learn about Jesus, too.

"Sorry you can't go," he continued.

He thought a minute. "Hey! I know what! If you can't go to Sunday School, maybe Sunday School can come to you! I tell you what. I'll listen real well on Sunday morning and then on Sunday afternoon I'll come over to your house and tell you what I learned. Okay?"

"Sure!" Chuck agreed.

The two boys walked on until they reached Chuck's front walk.

" 'Bye!" he called. "Don't forget to come over Sunday. Gramps and I'll be here."

Bert was true to his word. When Sunday morning came, he paid close attention while Mr. Sparks, his teacher, taught the Bible lesson. He even made some notes in the margin of his quarterly.

That afternoon Bert and Chuck sat in the Petersons' front room. Bert told Chuck about Jesus and Peter. He told him how

Jesus had stopped the storm when Peter and the other disciples were out in a boat. He told how Jesus had walked on the water and how Peter walked on the water, too, as long as he kept his eyes on Jesus and had faith in Him.

For the next two Sundays, Bert went to Chuck's house. He listened carefully to Mr. Sparks in the morning and told his friend what he had learned in the afternoon.

Still Bert wasn't satisfied.

"I'm not a very good teacher," he thought. "I'm going to see if I can't get Mom to help Chuck."

The next two Sundays Mrs. Higgins went along with Bert to Chuck's house. She went on the third Sunday, but then things began to come up so she just couldn't make it. First, there was out-of-town company. Then there was a special church meeting. Bert continued the best that he could, but he still wasn't satisfied.

The next Sunday at Sunday School, Bert talked with Mr. Sparks after class.

"I know it's a lot to ask of you," he said, "but I have a friend who is not a Christian. He can't leave home to come to Sunday School. Could you go with me to see him on Sunday afternoons?"

"Oh, Bert, I'm very sorry," Mr. Sparks apologized. "I have a standing date at the delinquent boys' home at 2 o'clock every Sunday afternoon. I will be glad to see what I can do about it, though."

Bert was disappointed that neither his mother nor Mr. Sparks could come, but he wasn't discouraged.

"Well, I guess I'm better'n nobody," he said to himself.

That afternoon he picked up his Bible and quarterly and headed for Chuck's house. When he got there, he noticed a station wagon parked out in front. After running up the walk and ringing the front doorbell, he waited for Chuck to answer.

The door opened and Chuck greeted him with a bright smile on his freckled face.

"Come on in," he invited. "Two men from your church are here. They just told me how I can be a Christian like you! Come on in and meet them!"

Bert followed his friend into the front room. Mr. Edwards and Mr. Brown, two of Mr. Sparks' friends, were sitting on the divan. They smiled at him.

"Hello, Bert," one of the men said, "we're glad to see you. We've heard some mighty fine reports about you. Mr. Sparks asked us to come here today to visit with Chuck and his grandfather. You've done a good job of showing them how a Christian loves his friends."

"Yes," the other man agreed. "Chuck has just accepted Jesus as his Savior. And it's mostly because you have shown so much concern about him."

"And, Bert, guess what!" Chuck interrupted. "I can go to Sunday School now! Mr. Brown and Mr. Edwards said they'd pick Gramps and me up in the station wagon and we both could go! Isn't that great?"

Bert just stood there and grinned. This was even better than he had hoped. He was glad he had done what he could for Chuck. Maybe it hadn't been much, but he knew now that God had used him. Bert was happy that He had!

Bible Story:

Who Is My Neighbor?

When Jesus was here on earth, He walked among the people, preaching and teaching and healing.

One day some of the people were talking with Him and a scribe asked Him a question. "Which is the most important commandment?" the scribe asked.

Jesus answered.

"Thou shalt love the Lord thy God with all thy heart, and with all thy soul, and with all thy mind, and with all thy strength; this is the first commandment. And the second is like, namely this, Thou shalt love thy neighbor as thyself" (Mark 12:30, 31).

"But who is my neighbor, Jesus?" the scribe asked. "Is it the man who lives next door? What if I don't have a neighbor?"

"Everyone has this kind of neighbor," Jesus said. "Let me tell you a story."

"One day a man was walking along the road from Jerusalem to Jericho. This man was minding his own business, when suddenly, from out of nowhere, some robbers jumped on him.

"They took his clothes and his money. They beat him up and left him lying beside the road, hurt and bleeding.

"The poor man could not get up, he was hurt so badly. He just moaned and groaned. Some of the time he was conscious, and some of the time he was unconscious and did not know what was happening. He was all bloody, and what clothes the robbers had left on him were ragged, torn, and dirty. It was obvious that he needed help and couldn't help himself.

"After the wounded man had been lying beside the road for quite some time, he finally heard footsteps.

" 'I'm glad someone is finally coming,' he said to himself. 'Perhaps they will help me.'

"Closer and closer the footsteps came. Finally, he could see that it was a priest who was walking along the road.

'A priest is a good man,' he thought. 'He will be sure to help me.'

"But, what's this? The wounded man couldn't believe his eyes. The priest had seen him. He was sure of that. But instead of coming over to help him, he had crossed to the other side of the road and was pretending that he had never seen him at all!

"The wounded man moaned. Perhaps someone else would come along and take care of him. He waited and waited.

"Pretty soon he heard footsteps again. He looked up and saw a Levite, a man chosen by God to serve in the temple. Surely the Levite would help him!

"But, no, the Levite, who was supposed to be a very special person chosen by God to do a very special work, did the same thing that the priest had done. He crossed over to the other side of the road, too. Then he pretended that he had not noticed the wounded man lying on the ground.

" 'What shall I do? If someone doesn't help me soon, I may bleed to death,' the wounded man thought. 'The priest and the Levite wouldn't help me. If they won't, who will? I will have to lie here and die.'

"He closed his eyes. After a while, he heard footsteps again. But this time he didn't even bother to look to see who was coming. 'No one will help me,' he thought. 'There's no use hoping.'

"Nearer and nearer the footsteps came. And then, they stopped. The wounded man opened his eyes. Standing above him he saw a Samaritan. The Jews thought that the Samaritans were not good people, but here was one who had stopped and was looking at him—a ragged, wounded Jew lying beside the road.

" 'Well, now,' the Samaritan said. 'It looks like you need help. You are hurt. Let me see what I can do for you.'

"The Samaritan went over to his donkey and got some oil and some wine and a clean cloth from his bag. He went to the wounded man and knelt beside him. He poured the wine and oil in the wounds and used the cloth for bandages.

"When he was through, he said, 'There, I've done all I can for you here. Let me help you over to my donkey.'

"He reached down and pulled the man up to his feet. He helped him over to the donkey. He helped him onto the donkey's back.

" 'We'll have to take you somewhere for you to go to bed until your wounds heal,' the Samaritan said.

"He took hold of his donkey's strap and led him down the road. After a while, the walking Samaritan and the wounded man riding the donkey came to an inn where people could stay overnight.

" 'Here is a good place for you,' the Samaritan told the wounded man. 'These are good people. They will take good care of you until you are well.'

"The Samaritan helped him off of the donkey and into the inn.

"That night the Samaritan and the wounded man stayed together.

"The next day, when it was time for the Samaritan to leave, he went up to the manager of the inn. 'I have to leave now,' he said. 'But I will leave my friend here until he is well enough to be on his way. Here is some money. If it is not enough, I will pay the rest the next time I am here.'

"The Samaritan left, leaving the wounded man to get well."

"Now," Jesus said, "who proved that he loved his neighbor?" Which one of these was the wounded man's neighbor? Was it the robber? The priest? The Levite? Or, was it the Samaritan?"

Can you figure out from this story who you think the wounded man's neighbor was?

PROGRAM 22
LEARNING SELF-DISCIPLINE
(New Year's Day)

Larger Scripture Lesson: Matthew 26:36-46; Mark 14:32-42; Luke 22:39-46

Scripture for Children's Church: Matthew 26:36-39

Object Lesson:

Self-Discipline Takes Courage

Object: A candy bar

This candy bar might cause some people a lot of trouble. It could even cause you a lot of trouble. It could make somebody do something he shouldn't do. It might make you do something you shouldn't do.

Suppose you were on a diet and were not supposed to eat candy. Suppose I gave you this candy bar. Suppose you took it.

Knowing that you shouldn't eat it, but wanting to eat it very much, would cause you to have a problem. Many boys and girls and grownups, too, might just go ahead and eat the candy. However, if you had self-discipline, you wouldn't eat it.

It is very hard to have self-discipline. Perhaps that is why so few people have it. But you can train yourself to do the right thing if you really want to. Ask God to help you and then get rid of your problem. If it is the candy, give it to somebody, or throw it away, but get rid of it. Each time you do the right thing, you will be that much stronger the next time. It takes courage and strength to have self-discipline. And when we have it, we are better people because of it.

Application Story:

Margie Makes Her New Year's Resolutions

"Resolutions are for adults! They're not for kids!"

"Why not? Why can't I make New Year's resolutions if I want to?"

"Because you'd never keep them! That's why!"

"Well, I'll show you!"

Margie stomped her foot. Benjie made her *so* mad. "He thinks I'm still a little kid," she pouted to herself. "Well, I just really *will* show him!"

Christmas was over and Margie and Benjie, her big brother, were helping their mother take down the Christmas decorations. They had been talking about what they were going to do on New Year's Day when somebody had mentioned resolutions.

It was true that Margie hadn't even known what the word "resolution" meant until Mother had explained that it was rules that people set up for themselves.

"A lot of people make a list of resolutions on New Year's Day because they like to wipe the slate clean and start fresh and new. Since January 1st is a clean page on a brand new calendar, it's a good time to start making changes for the good in some of the things we do," Mother said.

"What kind of resolutions could I make?" Margie wanted to know.

"Well, what are some of the things you do that you know you shouldn't do?"

"Like fussing when I have to dry the dishes?"

"Yes, that's a good one."

"And, like not going to bed when I'm supposed to?"

"Yes, that's another one," Mother said as she looked over the front room to see if they'd put away all the decorations. "We're through now. Why don't you go to your room and see if you can think of some more? I'd say five or six would be plenty to work on."

Margie went into her room and stretched across the bed. "Let's see, what are some more things that I do wrong? I don't always get up when I'm called in the morning. Sometimes I forget my lunch money and have to borrow from somebody and Daddy said that isn't good. That's four. I need at least one more. I know. Sometimes I don't come straight home from school. Now, that's five."

Margie got up from the bed and pulled a piece of paper out of her notebook. Very carefully she wrote down her resolutions. This is what she wrote:

1. I will not fuss when I am asked to do the dishes.
2. I will go to bed the first time Mother tells me to.

3. I will get up when she calls me in the morning.

4. I will remember to take my lunch money to school.

5. I will come straight home from school every day.

After she had finished making her list, Margie skipped into the kitchen to talk with her mother.

"Look, Mother," she said, "I have my New Year's resolutions. Are they all right?"

"Here, let me see your list," Mother said.

Margie handed it to her and watched her read it. Mother smiled and nodded her head. "This is a very good list, Margie. Do you really want to do all these things? It will be hard, but I know you can do them if you decide to."

"I really do, Mother. I want to show Benjie that I'm big enough to keep New Year's resolutions and, anyway, I should be doing all these things."

"All right, then. I'll help all that I can. But it will have to be up to you. You must practice what grownups call self-discpline. It means you must decide to do something and then you must exercise enough control over yourself to actually *do* it. Some people never have any self-discpline and consequently never accomplish much in life.

"Is it like doing my homework before I go outside to play?" Margie asked.

"Yes, that's it exactly," Mother answered. "You know you should do your homework first, but sometimes it's hard to do the right thing. Each time you do what is right, though, instead of what you'd really rather do, you become just that much stronger. And each time it gets a little easier to do the right thing."

"I hope I can grow strong like that," Margie said. "I'm glad Benjie teased me about New Year's resolutions, because I'm going to be a better person because of it. I just know I am! I think I'll start right now, and then when New Year's Day comes I'll already be stronger than I am now!"

Bible Story:

Jesus In Gethsemane

Jesus knew that the time had come for Him to be betrayed. He knew that the soldiers were going to come to get Him this very night. He knew that He was going to be taken to court and that He would be found guilty of something He had not done. He knew that He was going to be killed.

Jesus wanted to pray because He knew that He would need extra strength to stand all that He was going to have to go through. He needed to be alone with God.

Jesus and His disciples walked to the Garden of Gethsemane. When they reached the garden, Jesus said, "Stay here," to all of them except Peter, James and John. To them, He said, "Come with Me."

Jesus, Peter, James, and John all walked further. As they walked deeper into the garden, it became very quiet. Jesus turned to the three disciples He had brought with Him.

"Wait here for Me," He said.

Peter, James, and John sat down on the ground and Jesus went on still a little further. Then He knelt down to pray to God. There, on His knees, Jesus talked with God. He fell down on His face because He was in such distress. He knew that soon the soldiers would come to take Him away. He knew that they were going to kill Him.

"Oh, My Father," He cried, "if it is at all possible, please don't let this terrible thing happen to Me. I know that when I die for the sins of the people You will not be able to look upon Me. However, even though I want so desperately not to have to do it, I want to do Your will."

He got up, brushed the dirt off his clothes, and went back to where He had left Peter, James, and John. There they were, sprawled out on the ground, sound asleep.

Jesus said to Peter, "Can't you even stay awake for Me for an hour? Watch. And pray."

Jesus then went off again to pray by Himself. Again He said, "Oh, Father, please don't let Me suffer this terrible death. I don't want to have to go through this terrible experience. But, if it is Your will, I will do it."

Jesus went back again to Peter, James, and John. Again He found them sound asleep. He didn't disturb them this time. He just turned around and went back to pray once more. Again He said, "Please, Father, don't let this dreadful thing happen to Me. But, if You say it is necessary, I will do it."

Then Jesus went back once more to Peter, James and John. They were still asleep.

"It's time for us to go back now," He said to them. "The soldiers will be coming for Me soon."

Peter, James, and John got up from the ground and walked back with Jesus to where the other disciples were waiting. When they reached them, many people came running up to Jesus to grab Him and take Him away. Jesus had known that this would happen to Him. He knew that it was God's will. Even though He didn't want to do it, He went along with the soldiers because He knew that this was what God wanted Him to do.

Because Jesus was God's Son, He knew what was going to happen to Him. Jesus was also a man, and because He was a man, he felt terror and fear when the soldiers came for Him.

He had prayed and asked God for strength, and God had given it to Him.

PROGRAM 23
SHOWING LOVE
(Valentine's Day)

Larger Scripture Lesson: Ruth 1, 2

Scripture for Children's Church: Ruth 1:16-18

Object Lesson

Love Lasts Forever

Object: A wedding ring

This wedding ring is a symbol of love. When two people fall in love and get married, they use a wedding ring to remind themselves of the love that made them want to get married and spend the rest of their lives together.

Just as a ring is a never-ending circle, so true love is never ending. It lasts forever. God's love for us lasts longer than we can imagine. It lasts for all eternity.

In I Corinthians 13 Paul said that there are three great things: Faith, Hope and Love. But the greatest of these is love.

Application Story:

"By My Valentine"

During the next week would be Valentine's Day. Everybody in Betty's class always thought it was such a fun day. Betty looked forward to the valentines she might receive, too, but this year her father had been out of work because of a strike and Betty knew there wouldn't be any money for her to buy valentines. She wished she could just be absent that day, but she knew that wouldn't be possible, no matter how much she wished it.

"If I just had some red construction paper and some lacy paper doilies," she thought, "I could make everybody a valentine." But she didn't have any red construction paper nor any lacy paper doilies, and she didn't have the money to buy them either.

"Or, if I just had some white construction paper and a red crayon," she thought. She didn't have any white construction paper either. At least, not much. She did have a red crayon though.

"Oh dear," Betty sighed, "what can I do? I'd like to give everyone in my class a valentine. I'd like to give Mamma and Daddy one, too. It would make them feel better," Betty thought, "because they had been so upset about the strike. She knew how hard it was for them not to have any money."

For several days Betty pondered over her problem. Every night when she said her prayers she asked God to help her be able to give her friends and her Mamma and Daddy a valentine. "Please, God," she'd pray. "They don't have to be big ones. But I sure would like to be able to give them *something!*"

Then the day before Valentine's Day arrived, Betty was beginning to feel pretty glum. She went through all of her things and managed to find enough paper to make four valentines, at the most. But she needed 18 more. And that wasn't counting the one she wanted for Mamma and Daddy.

"If I can't give something to everybody, I don't want to give one to anybody," she thought. "I don't want anyone to think I don't like them because I don't give them one."

That day at school all of the other boys and girls were noisy and excited about the valentines that they had ready to put in the class's gay red box which they had decorated in crepe paper. They had worked on the box as a class project and it was really very lovely. Betty did so wish she had something to put in it.

"I have a valentine for everyone in the class," Jane whispered to Betty. "And I gave you the prettiest one of all!"

Betty didn't like to say she didn't have a valentine for anybody, so she just didn't say anything.

"Do you have your valentines all addressed?" another friend asked her.

"No," Betty answered, groaning to herself. She felt miserable.

After school, Betty didn't run home like she usually did. Her feet just sort of dragged all along the way. "What can I do?" she kept asking herself. It wasn't just because her friends were all giving valentines that she wanted to give them all one. It was because she really liked them and wanted them to know she did. She was afraid if they didn't receive a valentine from her that they would think she didn't, and that would be terrible.

"You give valentines because you love people," Betty was thinking. "I know God wants me to love people. So I can't understand why He doesn't help me give valentines to my friends."

Feeling hopeless and forlorn, Betty went into the room she shared with her older sister, Barbara. Barbara was too big to care about valentines. She was lucky.

Betty began to go through her treasures once more to see if she could find something. When she picked up the stack of Sunday School papers that she had carefully saved, an idea came to her.

"Would it work," she thought? "Why not? She'd do it!" A big smile broke through on Betty's face. She hadn't smiled for ages it seemed. But now she had something to smile about! Busily she set herself down at the table with the papers and her red crayon. Then she took her stack of cherished stories. She had saved them for years because she liked them so well. Now she was happy she had them to share with her classmates. They wouldn't have the stories already, she knew, because none of them went to her Sunday School.

Carefully she chose the right story for each one of her friends— the one she felt they would like the best. She took her red crayon and printed very carefully so she wouldn't mess the paper up. "Dear Jane, Be my Valentine," she wrote on the first one and signed her name. Then she drew a little red heart with an arrow running through it. "It's not bad at all," she said to herself happily.

Betty made one for each of her classmates. "They really make very nice valentines," she thought. "And they'll be something they can take home and read. They're really quite special!"

After she had prepared the valentines for her schoolmates, Betty made one for her Mother and Daddy. She didn't think they'd want one of her papers, so she cut them out a big heart on a piece of white paper and printed a poem on it:

> Dear Mamma and Daddy (it read):
> Valentines are given to those we love,
> And so I've made this one for you.
> Because there isn't anyone in the whole world
> That I love better than you two!
>
> Your loving daughter,
> Betty.

Betty was cheerful once more. She hummed a tune while she worked. And that night when she said her prayers, she thanked God for helping her to solve her problem, because she knew it was He Who had given her the idea for making her valentines. "And I love You, too, God," Betty prayed. "I guess I should have made a valentine for you, but you don't need one, do You? Because I've already given my whole heart to You!"

Bible Story:

How Ruth Showed Her Love

Elimelech lived in Bethlehem of Judea with his wife, Naomi, and their two sons, Mahlon and Chilon. Elimelech and his family were happy in Bethlehem.

However, a great famine came. It didn't rain for many days. The farmers were not able to raise enough food, so there was not enough to eat. Even if Elimelech had been rich he could not have secured enough food for his family.

So, one day he called Naomi and Mahon and Chilon to him.

"We will all starve to death if we stay here," Elimelech told them. "Let's pack all of our belongings and go where we can get food. Our God will go with us even to a strange country."

Elimelech, Naomi, Mahlon, and Chilon packed their belongings. They left Bethlehem and traveled to a country called Moab.

Moab had plenty of food for the people to eat. However, the Moabites did not worship the God that Elimelech and his family worshiped. They worshiped other gods—gods who were false and who could not do anyone any good because they were not living Gods like Elimelech's God.

After Elimelech and his family had lived in Moab for a while, Elimelech died. This left Naomi alone with her two sons. The two young men decided to get married. Mahlon married a young Moabitess whose name was Orpah. Chilon married a Moabitess whose name was Ruth. Mahlon, Orpah, Chilon, and Ruth all lived with Naomi.

They were happy living like this. Naomi loved her two daughters-in-law, and they loved her. They lived together for ten years. Then something very sad happened.

Both Mahon and Chilon got sick and died.

Naomi, Orpah, and Ruth were very sad. They missed Mahlon and Chilon. Naomi began to miss her old home in Bethlehem, too. Now that she had lost her husband and sons, she was very homesick. She loved Orpah and Ruth, but everybody here was a Moabite. She wanted to worship her own God with her own people. She grew sadder and sadder.

Then, one day, Naomi heard some good news.

"There is no longer a famine in Bethlehem," a traveler told her. "There is more than enough food for everyone now!"

Naomi knew immediately what she wanted to do. She wanted to go home. She wanted to go back to Bethlehem.

Ruth and Orpah and Naomi packed their few belongings.

They all started traveling toward Bethlehem. The journey was going to be hard for the women, because they had no men to help them.

After they had traveled a short distance, Naomi stopped. She looked at Orpah. She looked at Ruth.

She said, "Orpah and Ruth, I love you both dearly. In fact, I love you too much to take you away from Moab, which is your home. You have seen me off to a good start. Now I want you to return to the homes of your parents where you will be welcomed, I know. You won't be happy in a strange country living among strangers. We worship a God whom you do not know."

"You have been very good to me," Naomi continued. "But I want you to go back where you may find husbands and raise families."

"Oh, no, I don't want to leave you. I love you," Orpah answered.

"I love you, too, Naomi. Don't send us back. We want to go with you!" Ruth said.

"I think you should go back," Naomi answered. "You won't be happy if you go with me. I will be all right. Please go back to Moab."

Orpah kissed Naomi.

"All right. If you're sure this is what you want me to do," she said. "But remember that I love you."

She turned and left Naomi and Ruth.

But Ruth clung to Naomi.

She cried, "Oh, Naomi, don't make me go back. Please let me go with you. Let me live with you. Your people will be my people. And your God will be my God."

Naomi looked closely at Ruth. She saw that Ruth meant every word that she was saying.

"Ruth," she said, "if you are sure this is what you really want to do, you may go to Bethlehem with me. But it will be hard for you. It will be hard for us both."

"Your God will be with us," Ruth said.

So, Orpah went back to Moab and Ruth and Naomi traveled on to Bethlehem.

When the two women reached Bethlehem, Naomi's old home town, many people came out of their houses to greet them.

"Hello, Naomi. Welcome home!" they called.

"Is it really you, Naomi?" others asked.

"Yes, it is I," Naomi answered. "I have suffered much since I left here. Elimelech and Mahon and Chalon have all died. But I have brought back Ruth, who is my daughter-in-law. She has come all this way to a country that is strange to her to take care of me."

Naomi and Ruth made their home in Bethlehem. Ruth took good care of Naomi. She learned to love the God whom Naomi worshiped. God blessed them, and they had many happy years together.

PROGRAM 24
JESUS SAVES
(Easter)

Larger Scripture Lesson: Luke 24:1-12
Scripture for Children's Church: Luke 24:1-6a
Object Lesson:

The Book Of Life

Object: A birth certificate

When you are born into this world, your mother is given a birth certificate for you. Among other things, this birth certificate has your name on it, it has the date you were born, the place where you were born, and your parents' names.

Birth certificates are important because they prove that you are a citizen of a certain country. If you were born in the United States, your birth certificate would prove that you are an American.

You have to have a birth certificate when you start to school. If you should want to travel to another country, you have to have a passport. You can't get a passport if you don't have a birth certificate.

However, when you accept Jesus as your Savior and are born into the family of God, you don't get a heavenly birth certificate to prove you are a citizen of heaven. You get your name put on a list, though. This list is in a book in heaven and it is called the Book of Life. God writes your name in the Book of Life as soon as you trust in Jesus. When He does this, it proves that you are a citizen of the Kingdom of Heaven. And when your name is put on that list, God leaves it there forever!

Application Story:

Joey Becomes God's Child

Joey's heart beat with happiness. Inside, he felt a peace that was still new to him. He was all dressed and ready for school and was now looking out of his bedroom window. He appreciated more than ever the greatness and wonder of God.

Joey had always known that there was a God. He, like many other folks, had always taken it for granted that God had created the world. He had always believed that he belonged to God because God had made him. But now he knew differently.

God had made him, yes. Or, at least He had created the first man and woman, Adam and Eve. And when he had formed them, He had done it perfectly. Joey knew that he wasn't perfect, though. Just last week he realized why. Mr. Anderson, his Sunday School teacher, had explained it very carefully to him.

"When God created Adam, He made him in His Own image," Mr. Anderson had said. "And because he was made in God's image, he could think and feel and make choices. Man was very different from the other animals God made. He could talk with God. He had a spiritual nature like God's, as well as a physical one like the animals."

"Adam was placed in a beautiful garden," Mr. Anderson continued. "He was given a woman for a companion and a beautiful place to live. He had all of the food he could eat and plenty of clear, clean water to drink. And not only that, Adam could talk with God, who came every evening to visit with him."

"Remember I told you that one of the ways Adam was like God was that he could make choices?" Mr. Anderson had asked. "Well, Adam made a very bad choice. He chose to disobey God, and when he disobeyed God he brought sin into the world. There was a tree in his garden called the Tree of the Knowledge of Good and Evil. Adam was told not to eat any of the fruit of this tree. If he ate any, God told him that he would die. Adam chose to disobey God and he ate some anyway."

"What happened to Adam then?" Joey interrupted. "Did he die?"

"No, not pyhsically, but Adam was no longer perfect. Now he couldn't stay in the garden and be close to God. He had made a bad choice. He had let sin come between God and himself. And not only Adam would die spiritually, but all mankind would die because of him."

"How can God be good if He would let everyone die?" Joey had asked.

"God is good. And because He is good He made a way so we don't have to die. He made a way that gives us a chance to become a member of His family again."

"That Way is Jesus. Jesus was God's Son. He came to the earth to give mankind a second chance—a chance to choose Him for ourselves. We don't have to go along with Adam's choice. Now each person can make his own decision. Each one of us can continue to disobey God, like Adam did, or we can ask for forgiveness and follow Him.

"All through the Old Testament God promised His people that He would send a Savior," Mr. Anderson had told Joey. "And then, one day, the little Baby Jesus was born. Jesus was the Son of God. He grew up and preached to the people about how they could be God's children. Then some people who hated Him killed Him. But Jesus didn't stay dead. Because He was God, He was stronger than death. He came out of His grave, alive."

Joey tried hard to understand all that Mr. Anderson had told him. He had listened very intently.

"So, you see," Mr. Anderson went on to explain, "we are not God's children just because He made us. We become His children when we choose to obey Him and to follow Jesus."

Joey knew that he had done many bad things that God wouldn't like. He had told stories that weren't true to his mother, and one day he had even taken some money that didn't belong to him. He knew he didn't always do what he was told to do either. He said to his teacher, "What do I have to do to become God's child, Mr. Anderson?"

"Joey, you don't have to do anything because Jesus has already done it for you! He came to earth and lived a perfect life. He died for your sins and because He was sinless he conquered death. All you have to do is to believe in your heart that He did these things for you and accept Him as your Savior. Ask God to forgive you of all the bad things you have done and to let you become His child. When you do that, and really mean it, Jesus will come into your heart. In the Bible it says, "As many as received Him, to them gave He power to become the children of God, even to them that believe on his name. . ." (John 1:12) ."

"I want to be God's child," Joey said, his bright eyes gazing into Mr. Anderson's. "I love Jesus and want Him in my heart."

"Then let's bow our heads, Joey, and tell God so."

Right then and there Joey and Mr. Anderson had bowed their heads and prayed that Joey's sins would be forgiven and that Jesus would come into his heart.

Ever since Joey raised his head from that prayer, he had this good feeling inside of him. He felt so good that he wanted all of his friends and relatives to know about Jesus, too.

"Joey, it's time for breakfast," Joey's mother called from the kitchen.

"Okay, Mom, I'm coming," he answered as he hurried out of his bedroom door.

Soon breakfast was over and the school bus stopped in front of the house. Joey got on it and waved goodbye to his mother. After sitting down in his assigned seat, he turned to speak to his friend.

"Hi, Ralph. What'd you do last night?"

"Oh, nothing much. Just messed around and watched television. What'd you do?"

"After I did my homework I memorized a Bible verse. Want to hear it?"

"Why not?"

"It's found in John 1:12 and it says: 'As many as received Him to them gave He power to become the children of God, even to them that believe on His name.' "

"What does all of that mean?"

"It means just what it says—that if you believe in Jesus you can become a child of God."

"Aren't we all children of God anyway?" Ralph wanted to know.

"No. I used to think that, too, but Mr. Anderson, my Sunday School teacher, explained it to me last week," Joey said. He looked out of the window and saw that they had arrived at the school. "I'll come over to your house and talk about it with you if you want me to."

"Swell. How about tonight?" Ralph answered as all of the children filed out the door.

Jerry smiled to himself. It was beginning. Maybe before too long he'd be able to tell all of his friends about Jesus. He'd be glad when they all had the good feeling inside them like he did.

"I think I'll be a missionary," he said to himself, "and I'm going to start right here at home!"

Bible Story:

139

A Clean Heart

If we accept Jesus as our Savior, He will give us a clean heart.

Imagine that it's your birthday. You wake up bright and early, get dressed, and go to the kitchen for breakfast. Suppose you found a beautiful package in your chair when you pulled it out from under the table.

What would be the first thing you'd want to do? Why, open it, of course!

But just suppose you looked at it and said, "Who put this here? This isn't for me. I don't want it."

Somebody had loved you enough to get a present for you, to wrap it up, and to see that you got it. Whoever it was would be very unhappy because you acted the way you did.

That person wouldn't be the only one who suffered, though. You would, too, because you would miss out on the nice gift inside the pretty paper.

The package would still belong to whoever had bought it in the first place, because you hadn't accepted it.

So it is with the wonderful gift God has prepared for each of us. The gift of Jesus Christ, His Son. Unless we accept Him as our Savior, He can't come into our hearts.

Romans 6:23 says, "The wages of sin is death, but the gift of God is eternal life through Jesus Christ our Lord."

When we do accept Jesus, He washes our hearts and cleanses us from sin.

I John 1:7 says, "The blood of Jesus Christ, God's Son cleanses us from all sin."

Easter is a very special time of year. It's a time when you may dress up in pretty spring clothes. It's a time when the Easter Bunny may come to see you.

Actually, it is a special time because it's the time we set aside to remember the resurrection of Jesus. This was after Jesus had been killed and put into a tomb. He didn't stay dead. Easter is the time we celebrate Jesus' coming away from that grave alive. Because he had no sin in His blood, and because He didn't sin once when He was here on earth, He was able to overcome death.

When Jesus died on the cross it was a very sad day. His mother and some of his friends stood at the foot of the cross. They cried because they didn't want Jesus to have to suffer.

Jesus didn't have to suffer. He could have called hundreds of angels to come down out of heaven to take him off of the cross, but Jesus knew that someone had to save the people from their sins. He knew that He was the only One who could do it. He loved us enough to give His life for us.

After Jesus had died on the cross, a friend of His, Joseph of Arimathea, asked for permission to take His body and put it in a tomb.

Joseph very gently took the body of Jesus off of the cross. He carried it to his very own tomb which he had planned to use for himself. It was cut out of stone, like a small cave. He anointed Jesus' body and wrapped Him in a clean linen cloth. After he took care of Him, Joseph rolled a large stone to cover the opening of the tomb and went away.

The next day some priests and Pharisees reminded Pilate, the Roman governor, that Jesus had claimed that He would rise again on the third day. Pilate said, "We must be sure His disciples do not steal His body and claim that He has risen. Seal the stone in front of the tomb and station a guard before it."

The soldiers put wax on the space between the stone and the tomb and stamped it with the governor's seal. Then they stood outside of the tomb to guard it.

At sunrise the next morning, Mary Magdalene and Mary, the mother of James, went to the tomb. They were going to anoint Jesus' body with spices, which was a Jewish custom.

While the women were wondering how they could move the big stone that Joseph had rolled in front of the tomb, the earth began to shake. They were frightened.

An angel came down from heaven and rolled the stone away and then he sat on it. His clothes were as white as snow and his face was shining. The guards were so frightened that they began to tremble. Then they fell over, unconscious.

The angel said to the two women, "Do not be afraid. I know you have come to find Jesus. But He is not here. He has risen. Come see where the Lord did lay. You can see that He is gone. Then go and tell the disciples the good news."

The women ran as fast as they could to tell all of their friends the wonderful news.

Jesus had risen from the dead!

He had said He would, and He did!

Because Jesus had the power to overcome death, we can overcome death, too, through Him.

We cannot save ourselves, because we are not good enough. We have sin in our lives, but Jesus can save us. He will, if we just let Him.

PROGRAM 25
THE RESURRECTION OF JESUS
(Easter)

Larger Scripture Lesson: Matthew 27:57-28:20; Mark 16; Luke 24

Scripture for Children's Church: Luke 24:13-16

Object Lesson:

Eternal Life

Object: An Easter egg

Of all the holidays we have, boys and girls usually like Easter best, next to Christmas. Perhaps this is because we sometimes get Easter baskets. In the Easter baskets there are eggs—big eggs and little eggs, candy eggs and hardboiled eggs.

Have you ever wondered why we have eggs at Easter? It's because eggs stand for new life. Maybe you have seen a tiny baby chick. This tiny baby chick was first in an egg. The egg was kept warm until it was time for the chick to be hatched. When he got big enough and strong enough, he pecked away at the shell until the shell broke and he could climb out! The baby chick got its life from the egg.

Easter is a time when we think of new life because it is the time during which we remember Jesus and His resurrection. Jesus died on the cross, but He didn't stay dead. On the third day He rose again. He had new life.

If we accept Jesus as our Savior, we can have new life, too.

The next time you see an egg, remember how much Jesus loves you. Remember that He loved you enough to die for you. And remember, too, that He overcame death and made eternal life possible for you.

Application Story:

142

Skippy's Happy Easter

"Happy Easter!" The children's voices rang out. This was Thursday. Tomorrow was Good Friday and there would be no school. Everyone was in a holiday mood. At least, they all acted that way.

Even Skippy Adams acted like he was looking forward to Easter Sunday. And, in a way, he was, because Skippy was a Christian. He knew that observing Easter Sunday was the way Christians celebrate Jesus' rising from the dead after His death on the cross.

Skippy was grateful to God for sending His Son so he, Skippy, could live after he died, too. He loved Jesus and went to Sunday School and church every Sunday, not just at Easter like a lot of people did. In fact, his whole family always went together.

Skippy knew that this Easter would be hard for him, just like last Easter was. Most of the other boys and girls wore new spring outfits their folks had purchased for the special occasion. Some of the girls even wore hats, and some of the fellows sported new suits.

That was why Skippy was dreading this Easter. He knew he wasn't going to have any new clothes. He knew that his mother would have his best shirt and his best pair of jeans all starched and crisp, ready for him to wear. But he did so much want to own a suit like his friend Tom. "Wouldn't it surprise everyone," Skippy thought. "Yeah, especially me," he sighed.

"Hey, Skip, see you Sunday!" Tom called. "Want me to stop by your house for you?"

"I guess," Skippy answered. What else could he say? Then, "See you Sunday."

Skippy had eight brothers and sisters. It was a houseful, all right. A happy, exuberant houseful.

Skippy forgot about the suit Saturday as he and his brothers and sisters dyed the hard boiled eggs Mother had prepared for them. The aroma of vinegar and the sound of laughter filled the air as the children carefully dunked their eggs, one by one, into the colored dye. Skip, like the rest, was allowed two eggs. He took very special pains to make them pretty.

Saturday night found all of the Adams children preparing for the next day. The girls had shampooed their hair earlier, but the boys did theirs that night. Dirty bodies were scrubbed and toweled until they were red. Clean clothes were laid out for fast donning in the morning.

Skip looked at his yellow shirt and blue jeans hanging on the chair beside the bed he shared with his brother Sam. Nick slept in the small bed beside them.

Skip sighed. "Oh, well, I won't be the only one without a suit," he thought, "Sam and Nick will be there, too. But they're still too little to care, I guess."

Easter Sunday morning dawned fair and sunny. The weather was just right.

Skip and his brothers and sisters washed their faces, changed into their best clothes, and ate breakfast. Skip took time to plant a kiss on his mother's cheek. She smiled at him and gave him a loving squeeze.

Tom arrived just as everyone was ready to leave, and, just as Skip had expected, he was wearing a new Easter suit. It made him look tall and handsome.

"Your suit's swell," Skip said.

"Thanks. You look good, too," Tom said.

Out they all trooped. Four boys, counting Tom, and six girls, plus Mother and Dad. They looked like a small parade.

"You know, Skip," Tom said as the two boys took up the rear of the parade, "you're lucky."

"Me, lucky? Why, what do you mean?" Skippy wondered what Tom was talking about. "You got a new suit for Easter, and look at me," he blurted, looking down at his old yellow shirt and blue jeans. He just couldn't keep it bottled up inside any longer.

"Boy! I'd be glad to trade with you any day for what you've got," Tom answered. "Just look! Look at all the fun you have with your brothers and sisters. And you're going to church with your whole family, even your mom and dad. Me, I don't even have any brothers or sisters. And Mom and Dad are home arguing about some little old thing that doesn't amount to anything at all!"

"Yeah, I guess you're right at that. I just never looked at it that way before," Skippy agreed. "But I'll share with you, Tom. Mom says there are so many kids around the house anyway that a few more don't make any difference. Why don't you come over to my house this afternoon? I have two Easter eggs. I'd like for you to have one."

"Thanks, Skip. I'd like that. I'll bring my eggs over with me. It's no fun to eat them by myself anyway!"

The two boys grinned at each other.

144

"Funny thing," Skip thought, "it *is* a happy Easter. I was just too dumb to realize it!"

Bible Story:

For Forty Days . . . .

On Friday, Jesus was crucified. Joseph of Aramathea tenderly wrapped His body in clean, white linen cloth and placed it in a tomb which was a cave dug out of a huge rock. Then Joseph rolled a stone up into the entrance of the cave so no harm would come to Jesus' body.

On Saturday, the Roman governor had the stone sealed with wax and placed two guards in front of the tomb.

On Sunday, something very wonderful happened!

Early in the morning Mary Magdalene and Mary, the mother of James, came to put spices on Jesus' body.

As they were wondering how they could move the big stone to get inside the tomb, the ground began to tremble. It shook harder and harder. The stone rolled away from the entrance of the cave.

The soldiers were so frightened that they fainted!

The women were frightened, too, but they saw an angel.

"Don't be afraid," the angel said to them. "Look inside of the tomb and see what has happened. There is no body in the tomb! The Lord is risen!"

The two women were so happy they could hardly believe their eyes! They could hardly believe their ears! But it was true! Jesus was not in the tomb!

"We must tell the disciples!" they exclaimed.

They turned and started running to where the disciples were staying. As they were running, a man stopped them.

It was Jesus!

The two Marys dropped to their knees. They bowed their heads. They worshiped Him.

"I have a message for you to take to my disciples," He said. "Tell them to go to Galilee and I shall meet them there."

The women jumped to their feet. They ran to tell the good news to everyone.

A little later that same day, two men were on their way to the village of Emmaus which was about seven miles away from Jerusalem.

They were talking as they walked along the road.

"What strange things have been happening in Jerusalem," one of them said.

"Yes, indeed, everyone is talking about how Jesus has risen from the dead."

Just then a stranger came up to them and started walking along with them.

"What are you talking about?" the stranger asked the two disciples.

"You mean you haven't heard what has been going on in Jerusalem for the past three days?" Cleopas answered. "That's what everyone is talking about. Jesus of Nazareth was crucified last Friday. Today some women went to the tomb and He was no longer in it. He had risen from the dead! They saw Him and talked with Him in the garden. Others have checked the tomb, and sure enough, He is not in it. Only the white burial cloth is in there."

The stranger looked at the two men. "Oh, foolish men, why are you so surprised? Isn't it in the Scriptures that Jesus had to do all of these things and that He would then go to heaven?"

He quoted many passages of the Old Testament to show them what the Bible said about the death and resurrection of Jesus. He explained all of the verses to them.

Soon they reached their destination and the two men invited the stranger to come in with them and have something to eat.

They all sat down at the table. The stranger took the bread and blessed it and broke it and gave it to them.

Suddenly Cleopas and the other disciple realized who the stranger was. It was Jesus Himself!

But as soon as they recognized Him, He vanished. They could no longer see Him. He was gone.

They looked at each other.

"No wonder we felt the way we did when He spoke to us about the Scriptures!" Cleopas exclaimed.

Now they were too excited to eat. They jumped up from the table and hurried back to Jerusalem. They wanted to tell everyone what had happened to them!

When they reached Jerusalem, they burst into the room where the eleven apostles were staying. "We have seen Jesus!" they shouted.

"Peter has seen Him, too," the apostles said.

While they were all standing there chattering to each other, Jesus suddenly was standing right in the midst of them!

"What's the matter?" Jesus said. "Don't you know Me? I told

you I would rise again. Look at me! See, it's really me! I'm not a ghost. A ghost wouldn't have flesh and bones, but I do!"

While they were trying to gather their wits about them, Jesus said, "Do you have anything here that I can eat?"

Someone gave Him a broiled fish. Jesus ate the fish. He wanted them to see that He really was alive.

Another time, seven of the disciples were fishing in the Sea of Tiberias. They had been fishing all night and had caught no fish at all.

While they were still in the boat, Jesus stood on the shore.

He called to them. "Did you catch anything?"

"Not a thing," they called back, not knowing that it was Jesus.

"Cast your net on the right side of the boat and you'll catch some," Jesus said.

The disciples cast their net on the right side of the boat. When they tried to pull the net back up, it was so full of fish that they couldn't lift it!

"It's the Lord," Peter shouted. He grabbed his fisherman's cloak and jumped into the water and swam to shore.

The others followed in the boat, dragging the net full of fish. Peter ran to help pull the net in. The load of fish was very, very heavy, but the net did not break!

Once five hundred people saw Jesus at the same time. This was on a mountain in Galilee.

Jesus was seen by many people after He rose from the dead. He appeared on earth for forty days before he went to heaven to be with God.

PROGRAM 26
ON BEING JEALOUS
(Halloween)

Larger Scripture Lesson: I Samuel 17, 18

Scripture for Children's Church: I Samuel 18:7-9

Object Lesson:

Our Best

Object: Two papers which look like school examinations. Have them graded—one with 100% and one with 80%.

Here are two test papers. One was written by Jack and one was written by Tom. Jack's paper has 100% on it; Tom's has 80%.

When Tom gets his paper back from the teacher, he could react in several different ways. He could be glad that Jack got 100% and he got 80% because they both had done their best, or, Tom could be jealous. He could be angry because Jack got a better grade than he did.

Being jealous means that you aren't glad when somebody does better than you or when someone has something better than you have. Being jealous is wrong and it makes us feel bad inside.

We should always do the best we can do and not be sorry if somebody else does better. God doesn't want any more from us than we are able to give, but He does want us to do our best. If we've done our best, we don't need to worry about anybody else. God is the One whom we want to please. He knows what our best is!

Application Story:

Ruth's Halloween Party

Ruth Owens didn't even know what the word "jealously" meant. She didn't know it was wrong to be jealous, but Ruth was jealous, and she was wrong.

When you are jealous, it means that you don't like for nice things to happen to other people. You want them all to happen to you. You aren't happy when others have special talents or when they get any special attention.

Ruth couldn't play the piano at all, but Alice, a girl in her room at school, could play very well. Alice could play almost every song they sang at school. Ruth was jealous because Alice could play the piano so well. Because she was jealous of her, Ruth didn't like Alice very much, and she wasn't very nice to her. Of course, Ruth wasn't Alice's friend. No one wants a friend who is jealous!

Then there was Mary. Mary could paint pictures. Miss Newsome, the art teacher, was always showing Mary's pictures to the class. Ruth could paint pictures, too, but she could see that they weren't nearly as nice as Mary's. She wished Miss Newsome would say something nice about one of her pictures some time.

Jill was in Ruth's class at school, too. In fact, Jill made better grades than anyone in there. She was a good speaker and got to be in all of the school plays. So, of course, Ruth was jealous of Jill, too.

Margaret was a good writer. Her papers were always neat and clean and the letters all slanted in the same direction. Only the other day Mrs. Rich, their writing teacher, had complimented Margaret on her nice neat papers. So, of course, Ruth was jealous of Margaret.

Ann had a nice clear, soprano voice. She could sing so well that she was always asked to sing a solo if there was a special program at school. No one ever asked Ruth to sing a solo. Naturally, Ruth was jealous of Ann.

To tell the truth, it seemed that Ruth was jealous of everybody. Consequently, she was a very unhappy girl. She was lonely, too. She didn't have any friends, and, of course, you can see why!

One day Ruth's mother said to her, "Ruth, you are alone too much of the time. Why don't you ever have any girl friends over to play with you?"

"Oh, I don't know," Ruth answered. "I guess I just don't want to."

"Would you like to have a party?" Mrs. Owens asked. "I'd be glad to furnish the refreshments if you would."

A party? Ruth didn't know. "Sure, it would be fun," she guessed.

But who could she invite? "I don't know, Mother," she said. "I'll have to think about it."

Ruth thought and thought. What kind of a party could she have? It was three weeks until Halloween. Perhaps she could have a Halloween party. But that would be so much trouble," she thought.

"Mother," she said the next evening after school, "you told me I could have a party. Could I have one for Halloween? I think that would be fun, but I have a problem. It takes so much work I couldn't possibly do it all by myself. Would you help me?"

"Well, I said I'd furnish the refreshments," Mrs. Owens answered. "But you must do the rest. Perhaps you can get some of your friends to help you."

Ruth didn't answer her mother. She hated to say that she didn't have any friends.

"Let's see," she thought to herself. "What should I do to have a good Halloween party? First, I'll need to decide when I'm going to have it, and then I'll have to make out my guest list. Then I'll need to write and send invitations. We'll need to play some games and we'll need to have decorations and prizes. "Ruth's mind began to bubble over with ideas. "It'll be fun planning the party," she thought, "and maybe I can ask some of the girls to help me. It won't hurt to ask. All they can do is to say no."

Ruth decided to have the party the Saturday afternoon before Halloween and then she got busy with her guest list. Mother hadn't put any limit on the number she could invite, so she decided the best thing to do would be to ask all of the girls in her class at school. "That way I won't have to leave anybody out," she thought.

"Now, I'll have to write the invitations. Maybe Margaret will help me do that. She's a very good writer. And I'll ask Jill what I should say. She's so smart it'll be easy for her."

Mary was the first one who came to Ruth's mind when she thought of the decorations. "She can help me draw jack-o-lanterns and witches and goblins," Ruth thought. "And Alice and Ann can help with the games."

Ruth was getting more excited. She could hardly wait until she went to school the next day. As soon as she got there, she saw some of the girls talking together, and she did something unusual for her. She walked right up to them and said, "Hi!"

The girls all looked at her. They were surprised because they knew Ruth didn't like them. They wondered why she was so friendly now. "Hi!" they said as they moved back so they could include her in their circle.

"Guess what!" Ruth began. "My mother told me I could have a party, and you're all invited."

"Really?"

"That's great."

"When's it going to be?"

It was obvious that the others thought it was a good idea, too. Ruth was glad they had been so nice to her when she spoke to them. She knew she didn't deserve it. They all began chattering like little birds.

Soon the school bell rang and they had to postpone their planning until recess. Then they gathered together again and talked about their ideas and suggestions.

"Could you come over to my house tonight, Margaret?" Ruth asked. "And you, too, Jill. I'd like for you to help me with the invitations. Then the rest of you can take turns coming over so we can get everything planned. Is that all right?"

"I'll ask my mother," Margaret said. "If she says I can, I'll come over as soon as I change my clothes."

"Me, too," Jill said.

All the rest of the girls indicated that it was fine with them.

That night Margaret and Jill visited Ruth and the three of them worked hard. They were proud of the nice invitations they made.

The next night Mary went to Ruth's house and they worked on decorations.

The next night Ann and Alice came over and they planned games.

Each of the girls decided not to tell the others what they had done, so Ruth had all kinds of secrets with her friends. She and Margaret and Jill didn't tell the others about what they had written. She and Mary didn't let a peep out about the decorations, and no one but Ann and Alice and Ruth knew what games they were going to play. Oh, it was a lot of fun.

Ruth almost hated to see the day of the party arrive because she had such a good time planning it. Still she knew that she would enjoy it. She knew, too, that she would enjoy being with her friends. Suddenly she realized that she didn't have that ugly feeling about the other girls any more. She was glad her friends could do things, and she realized she could do things, too. After all, hadn't she organized the whole party? Ruth was glad her friends had helped her with it. And she was especially glad that now they were her friends!

Bible Story:

Saul, A Jealous King

"We want a king," the Israelites told the prophet Samuel. "All the other nations have a king. We want one, too."

Samuel knew that God didn't want His people to have a king, but the Israelites kept insisting.

"Let me pray about it," Samuel told them. "We'll see what God says."

Samuel went away where he could be alone. He prayed to God, "What shall I tell them?"

"Let them have a king," God told Samuel. "They are rejecting me, but I shall choose a king for them."

Samuel went back to the people. "God will choose a king for you. All of you go back home now."

God did select a young man to be king of the Israelites. His name was Saul. Saul was a handsome young man. He was so tall that he could see over the heads of all of the people.

Samuel said to the Israelites, "You and Saul must follow God. If you do, you will be blessed. If you don't, God will send thunder and rain upon you and He will punish you."

Samuel looked up into the sky. He called unto God. Samuel's answer was rain and thunder. God wanted the people to know that what Samuel had said was true.

Everyone was afraid.

"Don't be afraid," Samuel said. "Just serve God and remember that all these things have been given to you by Him. He will bless you if you follow Him. You'll only be punished if you disobey Him."

Saul was a good king for a while. He led the soldiers into battle. They won every battle that they fought. But Saul forgot that it was God who had given him the power to win. He forgot that it was God who was blessing him. He began to take the credit for himself. He became proud, and he disobeyed God.

Saul began to be troubled by an evil spirit. He would get very unhappy. He would get mean to his servants and yell and shout at them.

One day, one of Saul's servants said, "I know what King Saul needs. He needs to listen to some music. It would quiet his nerves and make him feel better."

"I know someone who plays the harp," another servant said. "His name is David. He is the son of Jesse of Bethlehem. He is the youngest of eight brothers and he tends sheep for his father.

The servants told Saul about David.

"Bring him to me at once," Saul said.

David came to the palace and he played his harp for the King. The music was so sweet and pretty that it did soothe King Saul's nerves. Saul began to like David. He made him an armour bearer and an officer in his army. He trained him to be a soldier. He even let David return to Bethlehem once in a while to visit with his family and watch over his father's sheep.

Three of David's brothers were in the army. One time when David was visiting his home, Jesse, his father, asked him to go to see how his three brothers were getting along.

David went to his brothers' camp.

While he was there, he heard of the huge Philistine by the name of Goliath who had challenged the Israelite army.

"I'll take on any one of you single handed," he bragged. "If I kill this one who accepts my challenge, the Philistines win this war. If he kills me, the Israelites will win."

The Israelite soldiers were afraid of Goliath. He was strong and over nine feet tall. Not one of them wanted to fight Goliath all by himself.

When David heard about Goliath, he was not afraid. He said. "I will fight Goliath. Goliath is defying the army of the living God. God will help me to overcome him."

Everyone though that David was foolish. His brothers wished he'd go home. David was young, and he hadn't had any real experience in fighting, but he knew that God was on his side. He picked up five rocks. He walked toward Goliath. He put one of the rocks in his slingshot. He had killed many wild animals this way while he was a shepherd. He whirled the sling above his head. Around and around it whirled. Then he let the stone loose. It flew through the air. On and on it went. At last it hit the startled Goliath right on the forehead. Goliath fell to the ground, unconscious. David and God had defeated the giant Goliath. Together they had won the battle with the Philistines.

The Philistines turned around and ran as fast as they could. The Israelites had won the battle.

The Israelites were so pleased with David that they clapped their hands and sang songs about him.

This made King Saul very jealous. He didn't want David to have any praise. He wanted it all for himself!

One day while David was playing his harp for the king, Saul threw a big spear at him. David jumped aside and the spear missed. Two times Saul tried to kill David like this, but both times David jumped away so that he wouldn't be hit.

Saul lowered David's rank in the army. He sent him out to do dangerous jobs, hoping that he would be killed. He had become proud and now he was jealous. He was unhappy and didn't enjoy any of the blessings that God had given to him.

After King Saul reigned forty years, both he and his son were killed in a battle. Saul had become a failure because he didn't remember what God had done for him. Saul had allowed himself to become a proud and jealous man.

PROGRAM 27
CHRISTMAS GIFTS
(Christmas)

Larger Scripture Lesson: Matthew 2:1-11

Scripture for Children's Church: Matthew 2:1, 2

Object Lesson:

Gifts

Object: A wrapped Christmas gift

It's fun to jump out of bed on Christmas morning and go into the front room to look under the Christmas tree. It's fun to look at the presents and check to see whose name is written on all of the different tags. Sometimes we even like to squeeze and rattle packages.

In some families, everyone takes a turn opening his presents on Christmas morning. Everybody waits while one person opens something. Then the next person opens a gift which has his name on it. After everyone has opened one gift, the first person gets to open another one, and so on around the circle until all the packages are opened. This way everybody gets to see everything that everybody else gets. It makes the opening time last longer, too!

Boys and girls like to watch when someone whom they love opens a gift which they have given to him. They think that is almost as much fun as opening gifts they have received.

One of the nicest things about Christmas is being able to give presents to people we love.

The greatest and best Christmas present that anybody ever gave to anybody else was given to us by God. He gave us Jesus because He loves us so much. When we accept Jesus, the gift that God has given us, He gives us eternal life as well as forgiveness of our sins.

God's gift is so wonderful that we can't begin to describe it.

The Bible says, "Thanks be unto God for His unspeakable gift" (2 Corinthians 9:15).
Application Story:

A Christmas Present

It was Christmas Eve. The gaily colored lights on the Christmas tree blinked off and on. The silver tinsel draping daintily on the branches looked like icicles after a thaw. Freshly baked animal cookies swung on green strings. Multicolored presents wrapped and tied with fancy bows surrounded the base of the tree. A pungent odor of pine filled the air.

It seemed as if Wendy Perkins had everything possible to make a little girl happy at Christmas. Anybody who looked into the living room of the Perkins house would think that everyone in the house was thinking about Christmas and anticipating the mysterious excitement of the holiday.

But Wendy wasn't happy. She moaned and groaned something frightful. She had her mother and her father and her two brothers pretty disgusted with her. No one seemed to understand, and no one really seemed to care, she thought—as if it mattered—there wasn't anything anyone could do about it anyway.

Greta, her best friend, had just moved out of town and it seemed as if all of Wendy's happiness and good times had moved along with her. Things would never be the same, Wendy knew. There'd never be another friend like Greta.

"Wendy, dear, you can't let it make you so unhappy," Mother said. "Life has many disappointments. We must learn to be thankful for all of the things that we *do* have."

"I know, Mother," Wendy replied. "But Greta was my very best friend. I'll never have another friend like her in all of my life."

"That's true, Wendy. But you'll have many more friends, and you can always be grateful for all of the happy memories with Greta. Cheer up, because Daddy has a surprise for you this evening!"

A surprise! Wendy loved surprises!

"Tell me what it is. Please. I won't tell Frank and Jack," she begged.

"No, we'll all hear about it at supper tonight. But you just cheer up, because you'll like it, I'm sure!"

All afternoon Wendy teased her mother for a hint of what the surprise was going to be, but her mother wouldn't tell her. "No, you just wait," she'd say.

Now it was almost time for supper and Wendy was helping her mother set the table.

"Oh, yes," Mother said as Wendy reached up for the plates in the cupboard. "Set an extra place, please."

An extra place! They were going to have company! Wendy loved company. "Who can it be," she wondered. "It couldn't be Aunt Evie and Uncle Frank. They would take two extra places. It couldn't be Uncle Paul and his family. Hm-m-," she thought, "one person." She couldn't think of just one person. Now Wendy was really mystified.

The clock struck six and Wendy heard the car door close. Running to the front door to greet her father, she stepped out into the chilly air. He had someone with him, and he was carrying a suitcase. Who was it? Soon Wendy could see that it was a girl about her own age, but she still didn't know who she was.

"Hi," Wendy said when her dad and the new girl got closer.

"Hello, Wendy. This is Susan. Susan, this is our daughter, Wendy."

"Hi," Wendy said again.

"Hi," Susan answered, smiling shyly.

"Well, come on in." Dad invited. "There's no use standing here on the porch."

Wendy opened the door and they all went inside.

"Here, I'll take your coat," she said to Susan.

Susan took off her coat and tucked her scarf in her sleeve and handed them to Wendy. Then she stooped over to take off her rubbers so she could leave them by the door.

"Who is she," Wendy wondered. "She looks nice, but where did she come from?"

Soon everyone was introduced and they went into the dining room to eat supper. "You may sit by Wendy, Susan," Mother said.

"I know you are all curious about Susan," Dad began after they had been seated and he had asked the blessing. "I wanted to keep her for a surprise, because she's sort of a Christmas present!"

A Christmas present? What did Daddy mean? Wendy looked across the table at her brothers, Jack and Frank. Even though they were older than she was, she could tell that they didn't know what the secret was either. They looked as baffled as she felt!

Daddy went on to explain. "Susan is the daughter of a very old friend of mine. Her daddy and I went to school together years ago. Just recently I heard that he and his wife were in a tragic accident last year and both of them lost their lives. There was no one to take care of Susan so the court put her in a foster home where she could be looked after. When I learned about Phil and his wife, I found out where Susan was staying and went to visit her. That was a month or so ago. When I went to see her, I thought she was a mighty fine girl. The home where she was staying was very nice, but I could tell that she wasn't too happy there. For, you see, she didn't feel like she really *belonged*."

"Oh, Susan," Wendy said. "That's too bad."

"Well," Daddy continued, "I got to thinking about our family and what would happen to you children if something like that happened to me and your mother. I thought how much I'd appreciate it if some friend of mine took you in and raised you for his own."

"Oh, Daddy," Wendy interrupted. "Do you mean Susan is going to STAY? For always?"

"Yes, that's what I mean. That is, if it is what everybody wants and if everybody will be happy about the arrangement."

Jack and Frank both grinned at Susan. "It's sure all right with us! Isn't it, Frank?" Jack said.

"Sure, why not?" Frank agreed.

"Oh, Daddy, do you mean it?" Wendy squealed. "You mean I'll have my very own friend living right here with us? We can both use my room. It's plenty big enough. And we both can even use the same clothes and she can play with my dolls and we can take turns on my bike. . . ."

"Wait a minute!" Daddy said. "I think you've all let me and Susan know how you feel. Now it's up to Susan. But we'll give her a little time to make up her mind. After all, she's just met us and she needs to know more about us. She's going to stay here over the Christmas holidays. I think she'll be able to make up her mind by the time she has to leave. Don't you think so, Susan?"

Susan smiled at Mr. Perkins. "I'm sure I can."

"Well, then, let's eat," Mother said. "Wendy, please pass Susan the potatoes."

Wendy handed the potato dish to Susan. She looked at her new friend. "I'm going to do my best to make her like us," she thought as she looked into Susan's eyes. "Here I was feeling sorry because a friend of mine had moved away and Susan doesn't even have a mother or a daddy or any brothers. She and I'll have great times together and she can share *my* family. I'll even share my Christmas presents! How lucky I am! I hope Susan likes it here at our house. I'm sure going to do my best to help her decide to stay."

"This is going to be a great Christmas!" Wendy said out loud.
Bible Story:

Wise Men Follow A Star

One night, long ago, the Baby Jesus was born in the little town of Bethlehem.

God had told many prophets that a Baby would be born some day and that this Baby would grow up to be the Saviour of the world. Seven hundred years before Jesus was born, a prophet by the name of Micah said that He would be born in the Town of Bethlehem.

Some of the people listened to the prophets. Some of them read what the prophets had written about the Saviour.

There was a group of wise men who lived in the East, in a country a long way from Bethlehem. These wise men were called astrologers, because they studied the stars. They knew that God had promised to send a Saviour, too.

One night, they were looking up at all of the stars twinkling in the sky. They were quietly studying them. The sky was especially bright and clear. The stars looked like diamonds sewed on to blue velvet cloth.

Suddenly, one of the men pointed upward.

"Look!" he said. "There is a new star tonight! See how big and bright it is!"

"I know what that star is!" another wise man said. "It is the star that is telling the world that the King of the Jews is born!"

"Let's go see Him! We can follow the star and find Him!" another one said.

The men gathered together the food that they would need for the trip. They packed the clothes that they would have to have. It would be a long journey, they knew, because the star was a long way off.

They put something very special into their bags, too. They very carefully wrapped gifts to give to the Baby when they found Him.

Soon they were all ready to leave. They climbed up on their camels and started their long trip across the desert.

Many weeks later, the wise men arrived at the palace of King Herod, who lived in the City of Jerusalem.

They said to the king, "Where is the Baby Who was born King of the Jews? We have seen His star in the East and have traveled a long way to worship Him."

King Herod did not know.

He called all of the chief priests and scribes to him.

"These men say that a baby has been born who is going to be king of the Jews. Where is this child?" he asked them.

"He is supposed to be born in Bethlehem," the scribes and priests told him. "We know this because the prophets have written this."

The wise men left Jerusalem that evening.

They looked up into the sky.

There was the star again! Just as big and bright as ever! And it was leading them to Bethlehem!

They were glad that Bethlehem was not very far away. They were getting anxious to see this wonderful Boy. They followed the star right into the little town of Bethlehem. The star seemed to hover directly over a certain house.

"This must be the place," they said.

They slid off of their camels. Each man very carefully got out his gift for the Child. They walked up to the house and knocked on the door. Soon, a man came to answer their knock.

"We have come to see the Child Who is born King of the Jews," the wise men said.

"Welcome," the man answered, opening the door. "Come with me."

They followed the man into the house. There, lying in a bed was the little Boy. He was so sweet. He smiled at His visitors, and waved His arms about.

The wise men knelt down right there beside Him.

They bowed their heads and prayed. "Thank You, God, for guiding us to the Christ Child. We know He is Your Son. Thank You for sending the big, bright star so we could find Him. We thank You, too, for letting us come to worship Him."

They rose to their feet. Then they looked over at Mary, the Baby's mother.

"We have brought gifts," they said.

They opened their bags and took the gifts out. They handed the presents to Mary. Mary took the gifts for her Son. She unwrapped one very slowly. She looked at it. It was a wonderful gift, and expensive. It was gold.

Then she opened the second gift. It was an expensive gift, too; it was frankincense, a very expensive oil.

Then she opened the third gift. "How lovely," she exclaimed as she looked at the spices. She smelled them, they smelled good!

"Thank you," Mary said. "These are very nice gifts."

"You are welcome," the wise men answered. "Now we must go. We have worshiped the King of the Jews and have given Him our gifts. Now we must return home."

The wise men were happy that they had been able to worship Jesus. They were happy that they had brought Him nice gifts.

Today, we give gifts to people we love. We like to do this especially at Christmas. This is the way we celebrate Jesus' birthday.

But the best gift of all to each of us is the Baby Jesus Himself. God gave Him to the world because He loves us so much.

John 3:16 says: "God so loved the world that He gave His only begotten Son that whosoever believeth in Him should not perish but have everlasting life."

The Wise Men

One night some wise men looked up at the sky.
"Look! Look!" they said to each other.
"Look at the new star up there tonight.
See how it seems to hover?
It's telling us of the Christ Child's birth.
What a wonderful star to discover!"
They packed their bags and got on their camels
   And soon were on their way.
They traveled at night so they could follow the star,
   And rested when it was day.
It took a long time to get to the place
   Where the star was leading them.
But it was worth the trip to see the face
   Of the Baby of Bethlehem.
They gave Him gifts and worshiped Him,
   They knelt beside His bed.
They prayed to God and said to Him,
   "To the Christ Child we've been led."
They gave Him gifts to show their love,
   And we give Him gifts today.
We can show our love by helping others,
   And we can also pray.
We can worship Him by singing songs
   And listening to His Word,
By being nice and still in church
   So the preacher can be heard.
We thank Thee, Lord, for telling us
   The story of these men.
Help us now to show our love
   Just as they did then.